PARTY LIKE A
ROCK STAR

PARTY LIKE A
ROCK STAR

A Celebrity Party Planner's Tips and
Tricks for Throwing an Unforgettable Bash

jesGORDON

with
Jessica Baumgardner

life

Guilford, Connecticut
An imprint of The Globe Pequot Press

This book is dedicated to Linda Satz, who started this whole mess, my grandmother Rose, the coolest lady in Heaven, and my husband, Bill, (affectionately known as Mashkie). You make all of my dreams come true.

To buy books in quantity for corporate use or incentives, call **(800) 962-0973** or e-mail **premiums@GlobePequot.com.**

GPP Life is an imprint of The Globe Pequot Press.

Text design by Sheryl P. Kober

Library of Congress Cataloging-in-Publication Data is available on file.
ISBN 978-0-7627-5142-6

Printed in China

10 9 8 7 6 5 4 3 2

CONTENTS

From Jes Gordon

Thanks to my family: Dad, yes, we can! Mom, you taught me that it's not how smart you are, it's *how* you are smart; Maggie and Al, you complete all of us; my big bro, you always say it better than me; and my pets, Hurricane, Ruckus, and Bella.

I would like to thank those who contributed to this book: my clients who inspire and teach me every day; Andre Maier, photographer sensation; David Pfendler; lighting and AV master Doug Jastremski from Power Posse Productions; Glenn Harris; Heathe St. Clair; Suzanne Gillam from The Catering Company; and Audrey Woollen from Urbanic Designs. Thanks to my coauthor, Jessica Baumgardner, who helped make sense of it all, and to our agent, Jennifer de la Fuente at Fountain Literary, as well as Frank Scatoni at Venture Literary.

A special thanks to my staff past and present with gold stars next to Ruth Mikos, Natalie Taylor, Janna Ferner-Bell, and Tracy Rohrer. Thanks to my dear friend Tracey Sarn, wonderful venues such as TriBeca Rooftop, my vendors who just simply "get it," and all the freelance designers who make me look good—with an extra shout-out to Frank, Laura, Louis, Elizabeth, Randi, Shelly, and Diann.

From Jessica Baumgardner

Thanks to Jes Gordon for making this writing thing fun; my family, especially my chef sister, Andrea Baumgardner, who shared her extensive knowledge of food and wine; and my husband, Irad Eyal, who went to the playground a lot so I could work.

How to Have Fun at Your Own Party

Once upon a time, I worked with a bride who was a monumental pain in the ass. She was loud, intimidating—and completely miserable. This girl always had a scowl on her face. I'd offer a suggestion and she'd shoot it down. I'd ask her a simple question such as, "What color do you like?" and she'd bark back, "I don't know."

I've had clients like her before. They act like they are embarrassed to answer incorrectly and they don't want to be held to their decisions. Their attitude is, "You're the designer, you tell me what my favorite color is!"

The bride claimed that nothing inspired her, that she wanted her wedding to look exactly like a certain magazine spread but also totally original. Honestly, there were times I considered handing her over to a competitor in the industry, but I knew I should be a grown-up and follow through. Also, I figured that because she could find at least one person to love her, she deserved to be honored.

Event planning is like therapy, and I'm the Dr. Phil of party planners. I try to uncover my clients' innermost desires, what their favorite things were as kids, and build from there. This bride was

A ceiling that's a little bit country. ANDRE MAIER PHOTOGRAPHY

focused on having a kick-ass New York City wedding. Many of her socialite friends had gotten married recently and her mind was cluttered with their choices. I realized my job was to help separate her from the rest of the world. Those other weddings had nothing to do with her, so we cleaned the slate. And once we got rid of all her emotional baggage, she actually turned out to be a creative, beautiful person.

She loved the English garden look, but was into the slick urban thing too. So we designed a wedding that was a little bit country, a little bit rock and roll: a modern all-white venue dripping with a verdant ceiling of vines, moss, and flowers. Their feet were grounded in the city but their heads were in the clouds. We had a bluegrass band for the cocktail hour and a funky Motown band for dinner and dancing. She felt like a star—and all her skinny socialite friends loved it. After all the trauma, her wedding ended up being spectacular.

And that's why I wrote this book—I want your parties to be spectacular, too. I want you to be able to express yourself in every celebration you host, and I want to give you the inside scoop on how to do it right so you can achieve the impossible—having fun and feeling like a rock star at your own party. And this isn't about having Mick Jagger's budget either. You can incorporate edgy, over-the-top elements into everyday celebrations, like making vinyl appliqués out of photos of the birthday girl and wallpapering the whole room with her image. Or making custom piñatas for a baby shower out of papier-mâché—it's easy to do, easy on the wallet, and expresses something more personal than your average donkey. I once had a cake made for a client's birthday that was a sculpture of him lazing on the couch, watching the boob tube, and reading *Golf Digest*—weirdly enough, he loved it!

Every event I design has a part of me in it. I have a style unlike

A Warhol-esque vinyl appliqué glammed up this bat mitzvah.
ANDRE MAIER PHOTOGRAPHY

the other WASPs and gay boys in this business. If Martha Stewart is posh suburban Connecticut and Colin Cowie is West Palm Beach, I'm NYC street: a little funky, a

Even your dinner table can express your personal style.
ANDRE MAIER PHOTOGRAPHY

I specialize in helping people express artistically who they are intrinsically, instead of just copying the trends. I may not be good at many things (like balancing my checkbook or cooking dinner) but this is an area I've excelled in—or so I'm told.

Party Like a Rock Star is about entertaining and lifestyle, but more important, it's about you. So many people don't have the confidence to be assertive about what they like or don't like. They can dress themselves and they can order their favorite dish off a menu at a restaurant, but when it comes to planning a party, they're like a deer in headlights. Also, parties are supposed to be all champagne and sweetness and light; in reality, throwing a bash pushes the calmest of hosts to new heights of neurosis and panic. Why does it seem so difficult to enjoy an endeavor that's supposedly all about enjoyment? Having to organize an event, in front of all your friends and colleagues, with perfectly prepared

little gritty, but fun and surprisingly accessible.

Even though I've been planning events for twenty years, I never get bored. Party after party, it's never the same experience. No matter how many times I set tables or drape crushed organza, when I see the reaction from my clients, I'm surprised and giddy all over again.

food and sparkling drinks and raucous entertainment and fire extinguishers—whew! You can see why people hire professionals to help them out. This book will be your party planner stand-in. My job is to give you the courage to find your style, but I won't be defining it. I also don't want you to play it safe— you can be wildly creative while still hitting the sophisticated and high-quality mark. Basically, I want to show you how to create a world of glamour at your event but still feel at home. This industry is desperate for an honest, in-depth, and easy-to-follow guide on celebrating, and that's what I've written. There is a lot of information out there on this particular subject—some of it is great, a lot of it is bullshit, but none of it is complete. I for one am tired of gazing upon glossy, picture-laden coffee-table books about entertaining that have a lot of beauty but not a lot of substance. It's fun to look at the eye candy, but do regular people have any way of achieving it?

My goal is to deliver reliable tips to anyone who needs them: a bride searching for inspiration when planning her dream wedding, a socialite who hopes to outdo her friends, a celebrity who wants to throw a quietly fabulous affair, and anyone else who is simply looking for a reason to party down. This book is for the person who loves to give dinner parties for her friends but is sick of the same old crudités plate and iPod mix. Or the person who is splurging on a huge birthday party for his mom, and he wants to do the night up right.

The occasion really doesn't matter; you can make an event out of anything you want. One of the most moving nights of my career was a party for Smokey Robinson and Berry Gordy Jr. to celebrate fifty years of being best friends—a relationship that survives that long deserves to be celebrated!

HOW TO USE THIS BOOK

Party Like a Rock Star is a user-friendly sourcebook for the world of

Party planning applies to celebrations of any size, from dinner parties to big bashes. ANDREW BICKNELL PHOTOGRAPHY

event planning, like an encyclopedia of entertaining. Most party planning guides are organized by the type of gathering—Christmas brunch, New

Some insider tricks that'll make your party pop. DAVID PFENDLER

and provides further details for those of you who really want to know more about, say, fishing wire and its myriad uses. Throughout the book, I have tried to refrain from regurgitating the tried, true, and tired tips about how to make a pretty centerpiece out of mini gourds—I want to give you my behind-the-scenes event-insider secrets involving gaffer tape, aluminum foil, and the playlist sure to get your guests boogying on the dance floor.

After surviving in this industry for as long as I have, I want my clients and everyone else to be able to get all the answers they need from one place. I want *Party Like a Rock Star* to cover all the factors that any host is going to have to think about when planning an event, large or small. Of all the productions I've launched, this is the mother ship.

Year's Eve cocktail party, spring bridal shower—but not this one. Chapters 1 through 10 provide a timeline of basic party planning elements from start (devising a concept and determining a budget) to finish (mouth-watering menus and hostess etiquette), with key industry words appearing in orange. The text is sprinkled with useful ideas in the form of SUGjesTION sidebars—easy to read, easy to implement. The glossary contains those terms highlighted in orange

CHAPTER ONE

Why Do This Thang?

The first and most important question I ask my clients—more important than budgets or location or food or guest lists—is, simply, *Why?* Before planning any event, whether it's a birthday party, bridal shower, or a casual get-together with friends, it's crucial that you ask yourself why you want to get into this mess in the first place. I assure you, if it's for the right reasons, it will be worth it.

So what's the right reason to throw a bash? Simply, you have something special to celebrate or share with a chosen group of people. An event can also be a wonderful tool for social or business networking, and it's a confidence booster to "run" a room. When you feel proud of the beautiful space or proud of your friends and are looking forward to introducing them to one another, a party can be the thrill of a lifetime (or at least a few weeks).

Think: You are tightening up the degrees of separation in this lonely world by bringing your friends together. I know many hosts who are happily responsible for business partnerships or even marriages because of introductions at their parties. Also, is it so horrible to have something to look forward to? It's nice to know that in the future you will be seeing people you enjoy. If you have this attitude going into planning an event, the party will no doubt be successful.

You need to start with the right reasons, because, let's face it, planning parties can be a pain in the assets. Often during dinner conversations, the guests ask me why people spend so much money on events. (That's simple—so I can buy more shoes!) But seriously, only a small percentage of folks are spending exorbitant amounts on anything these days. But even the smallest parties will put a dent in your budget, so this is why your desire to plan an event is so important.

Parties take time and effort—not just for you but for your guests too. People get dressed up, wear painful shoes, apply that once-a-year eye shadow, don a tie, iron the hair, and so on. Good reasons for getting together will not only make it worth your time but your guests' time as well.

It's easy to get into it for the wrong reasons, however. We've

all been wangled into planning a coworker's baby shower, a going-away dinner for friends, a charity event, and on and on. Many times people feel obligated to throw parties because of social pressure rather than from their own sheer desire. I've heard a bunch of wrong reasons over the years, à la: "Mrs. Schwartz threw an amazing **ladies' tea** last week and I want to show her I can do better." "I want to get laid." "I want to raise money for my new beach house." "I want my child/husband/wife to love me again." "I want to be featured in a fancy magazine." "I want to get wasted." "I want to have an excuse to redecorate my house." "I am bored." (Then again, if you have the money, go for it!) "I want to dress up and look fabulous and make all my friends jealous." "I want to order people around."

Other times, people get so caught up in the pomp and

A refined ladies' tea is not about competition. ANDRE MAIER PHOTOGRAPHY

Maybe it's just me, but cupcakes are the universal party G-spot. DAVID PFENDLER

From time to time we will all be thrown into the shark pond of entertaining against our will. Let's say you've been deemed the "chosen one" to throw your sister-in-law's baby shower, even though you sort of hate her. Or say you're the designated party thrower in your office for birthdays and going-away fetes, like Angela on *The Office*. That's when you need to take a step back and make those wrong reasons right. To do that, you need to find your party G-spot—the good part of this event that actually appeals to you despite its forced nature. If you adore babies, focus on all the cute baby stuff you can decorate your living room with, and that'll get you through the rough patches. If you're passionate about cupcakes, focus on cupcakes—and most likely your guests will have no inkling of your inner ambivalence. If you always gravitate toward the dance floor or the buffet table at other events, then

circumstance of an event, they forget the deep and real reasons why they are throwing a party in the first place. This disease particularly afflicts the soon-to-be married. Often when I'm in wedding planning sessions with a bride and groom, I have to snap them out of all the pretty white details and remind them: All this is about a *marriage,* not a *wedding*.

Jes, all dressed up as a professional party planner. ANDRE MAIER PHOTOGRAPHY

you know your party G-spot is all about booty shaking or yummy hors d'oeuvres. Your passion for this part of the party will spread to your guests and be felt throughout the event. This signature will be what everyone remembers because you actually cared enough about it to do it right.

Being a great host is about making everyone at your event happy—when everyone is partying effortlessly, that's when you feel like a rock star. If you thrive on making people happy and sharing your own happiness with others, or if you feel passionate enough about a cause to scream about it from the rooftops, then throw a bash. But what if you are the type of person who communicates best with your four-legged friends? If you're not a people person or you get tense and stressed out when you invite friends over for dinner, there are things you can do to turn yourself into a great host. Anyone can throw a spectacular bash—you just have to figure out whether you want to deal with the details.

DECISIONS, DECISIONS

One of your first decisions should be whether to hire someone to help you get through the process. This will obviously incur an added expense, but it might very well be worth it depending on the scope of your event. Here's one way to help you decide. Write out a basic, preliminary to-do list as if you were handling everything yourself. By putting the tasks on paper, you'll know if you have that DIY spirit. For instance, you desperately want to throw a big birthday bash for your best friend, but you've got two little kids and a full-time job—how much time in the day do you have left to plan a frigging party?

An enormous amount of detail goes into executing fabulous ideas, and there is a lot of help to be had out there. When you decide on your party budget, maybe forgo the million-dollar dress you had planned to wear (make it a half-million-dollar gown instead) and hire some support! The world is full of event planners, caterers, florists, entertainers, valet attendants, security guards—you name it. You can choose an area of particular craziness for you and hire a professional to help with just that (like a caterer for an extravagant holiday party) and still tackle the not-so-horrible parts yourself.

This "Do I want to deal with it?" question can also help you determine the scale of your event. Let's say you have delusions of grandeur and you'd like to throw that dream golf tournament for your father's seventieth birthday—along with fifty of his closest friends—but after getting the exorbitant price list from the club manager, all you can remember is good ol' dad not giving you the keys to the car when you were sixteen. You decide to take it down from fifty guests to a perfect ten—so the golf tournament birthday becomes a casual outdoor lobster boil. That's OK! Not every party has to be the next opening of the Taj Mahal. We are all paying mortgages, raising kids, going to work or school, trying to stay thin, and have many other responsibilities, so why not

keep entertaining in the small and simple category? The simpler you make your event, the more relaxed and fun you will be as a host, and that energy is infectious to your guests.

At times you will start out enjoying the planning process, and then when you are knee-deep in it, you start to feel trapped in party quicksand. Parts of the planning will be really annoying—such as seating arrangements, budgeting, and so forth—so when you feel yourself getting bogged down, try to visualize the magnificent finished product. Take a virtual tour of the upcoming party in your mind, imagine all the guests having a wonderful time, and

hopefully this will remind you why you are going through this shit in the first place.

• • •

I think the art of celebration is one we should all learn to master, and I'm here to help you with your schoolwork. When you decide to throw a party, approach it calmly, honestly, and with conviction. Be prepared to ask yourself, "Are you ready to plan this party with everything it entails?" And then get up on the bar and yell, "Hell, yeah!" Let's get started.

CHAPTER TWO

Right on the Money: Making a Budget

It's hard to put a price tag on celebrating—for many, parties are emotional, sparkly, happy things that shouldn't be associated with a dollar value. Besides, budgets feel so nerdy and overly practical, but they are instrumental in keeping your feet planted firmly on the Earth's surface. Budgets don't let your fantasies overtake reality. Throwing a party will cost money, but your net worth isn't the only thing that will make or break the event. The art of budgeting means always keeping a healthy perspective, avoiding rash decisions, and compromising on things that aren't necessary—really, the same kind of mental tricks that go into a good marriage.

CHOOSING THE CHUNK OF CHANGE

First, you need to come up with a number. Attend the dreaded meeting with the boss or go to the brunch with the in-laws or perform the gratuitous lovemaking session with your partner to find out exactly how much they are willing to spring on your event. If you are flying solo on this one, be absolutely firm with yourself about what you can manage. Again, the number doesn't really matter as much as your *sticking* to that number.

You don't have to have tons of this to throw a party, but you do need a budget, no matter what.
DAVID PFENDLER

Just because you are throwing a party, it doesn't mean that all your money needs to be magnetically attracted to this spot. That's why it's a good idea to keep a separate budget or even a separate bank account specifically for your event, and don't let that budget intermingle with your mortgage payments or children's college funds; in the heat of planning, it is all too easy for those boundaries to blur. When opening a celebration account, try to open one that earns interest in case of miscellaneous costs.

Please realize that the event itself is only part of the budget—you have dresses to buy, makeup to sample, invitations to design, toiletries to stock, a tan to fake . . . the extras can be mind-boggling! To get your head around this headache, try to visualize all the costs that could occur by simply making a grocery list of items needed in order to pull off a kick-ass party. Don't just write down "beer, burgers, birthday cake"—include *everything* on this

---

A TEMPLATE FOR BUDGETEERS!

1. Venue

a. Location fees: room rental charge, per head fee, plating charge, corkage fee
b. Home party fees: cleaning costs like surface cleaners, paper towels, bleach, maid service before and after event
c. Bathroom amenities: plungers, toilet brushes, room spray, candles, incense, tampons, toilet paper, hand towels, hand soaps, breath mints
d. Dinnerware (hardy plastic or paper is acceptable), glassware, napkins (allow five plates/glasses/cocktail napkins per guest—you'd be surprised how many of these people go through at a party), silverware, coasters, extra tables, table linens, serving platters
e. Outdoor maintenance: gardening, landscaping, walkway lighting
f. Trash bags, fire extinguishers, ashtrays or sand buckets
g. Designated parking: orange cones, valets
h. Coat-check people
i. Security
j. Air-conditioning/heaters/fans
k. Portable restrooms

2. Food/Drink

This section can vary, obviously, depending on whether you're serving a five-course meal, a casual buffet, or passing around appetizers on trays. Some possible expenditures may include:

a. Placed nibbles (nuts, olives, cheese), hors d'oeuvres, main courses, desserts
b. Cooking equipment, such as a grill, charcoal, lighter fluid, gas, cute grilling apron and hat (a must)
c. Caterer, waitstaff, tipping for servers
d. Food delivery/pickup
e. Alcohol: beer, wine, champagne, hard liquor, juice, soft drinks, bottled water, bar condiments, ice, bar tools, coffee, tea, bartender, tipping for bartender

3. Entertainment
   a. CDs, iPod
   b. DJ
   c. Live band (ask for a technical rider for any extras)
   d. Equipment: extra cables, speakers, surge protectors

4. Decor
   a. Throw pillows, slipcovers for sofas, furniture rentals
   b. Indoor lighting: lightbulbs, candles, disco balls, stepladder for overhead lights
   c. Flowers, hanging plants, florist services
   d. Outdoor lighting: tiki torches, stringed lights, paper lanterns
   e. Tent
   f. Balloons, confetti, banners, signs

5. Invitations
   a. Save-the-date cards
   b. Design costs
   c. Stationery
   d. Printing or calligraphy
   e. Mailing labels
   f. Postage
   g. Thank-you notes

6. Miscellaneous Costs
   a. Your beauty budget—party clothes, trips to the salon, and so on
   b. Photography/film costs
   c. Transportation for the tipsy
   d. Insurance and permits
   e. Parting gifts

list, from your preparty manicure to extra toilet paper to postparty cleanup, because those little costs add up.

After you've made up your projected list of expenses, now's the time to be brutally honest with yourself about your budget, and stick to your guns. If you are not honest about your budget from the beginning, you'll be disappointed when you can't afford those mini black-and-white cookies or when you end up with a live chipmunk band instead of the horn-blaring funk band you wanted. If you decide to hire vendors for your event (like a caterer or florist) and you underestimate the amount of money you'll be spending on them, the situation could get uglier than a World Wrestling Entertainment bout.

If you sign contracts with outside vendors (as opposed to your rented venue's in-house vendors), you are liable to pay the contracted amount. So be realistic about your budget and don't be embarrassed by the amount—that is simply a waste of time. There is nothing wrong with a small budget—it just means you may have to compromise on some things. Big budget or small budget, you are lucky to have a reason to celebrate, and making your grand entrance on the back of an elephant should not supersede that.

Don't blow your wad in one area only. Use the categories from my Template for Budgeteers (venue, food/drink, decor, etc.) and try to use equal percentages for each category. Try to allocate your budget evenly, as if you were spreading a perfect schmear of cream cheese on a bagel. A successful event is one that shines in every area. For instance, if you have a budget of $10K, it would be safe to assume that you should not spend $9K on catering.

GETTING DOWN TO THE NITTY-GRITTY

Next you need to figure out how much the things on your list are really going to cost. For the average

Keep your eye on food costs, but don't skimp on quantity.
ANDRE MAIER PHOTOGRAPHY

Joe or Jane, this can be hard to estimate. How do I know how much things cost? Well, Sunshine, it's called research. The phone and Internet are wonderful tools. Google your desired items—even better, Google them with the word "**wholesale**" and see if the prices are cheaper that way. It is a powerful feeling to compare prices and shop intelligently—it gives you confidence and control over your

event and prohibits that morning-after, resentful feeling of "Oh God, what did I just do?" When you get quotes for items, ask if these quotes include delivery and pickup charges, setup fees, fuel charges (which are becoming increasingly popular), and, of course, sales tax.

When tallying your projected food costs, remember that it's better to overbuy than underbuy. Nothing is as disappointing as stingy portions

Make sure to account for tips for waitstaff! ANDREW BICKNELL PHOTOGRAPHY

at a party. If you have leftovers, the worst-case scenario is to send guests home with doggie bags or donate all of it to a local homeless shelter. So instead of only having on hand one burger per guest, I would have two per person to be on the safe side. If you are throwing an event for the local football team, then up the ante. Sometimes your local liquor store will let you pay for your alcohol based on consumption—that is, if you have unopened bottles after your party, you can return them like an unwanted wedding present! Buy enough alcohol to allow each guest to have two to three drinks in a three- to four-hour period. Some people will drink more than others and somehow the supply always evens out. This is a good equation to keep in mind because you don't want to be liable for slobberingly drunk people—don't have the drinks flowing *too* readily.

If you've hired anyone to help you with your event, be sure to allocate some of your budget toward tipping. Money talks, so even if a dear friend has taken it upon herself to help you out, consider tipping or giving gifts to any helpers.

Tipping is just sending out good karma by thanking those people who made you look great. Many folks find it uncomfortable to give money to people they know, even if they are in a working relationship. They think that giving someone last season's Hermès scarf is a wonderful gesture, but on the average, people truly do prefer money. So get over yourself, stuff a check into an envelope, stick it in the mailbox, and make someone's day. Here's a list of tip-worthy folks you might have at your party: waitstaff, including bartenders, hosts, maître d's; the salesperson who helped you secure the venue if you are renting space; busing staff; cleaning staff, restroom attendants; entertainers, such as the band or DJ; photographer; florist; and the party planner and staff if you choose to hire a planner. If you are partying at home, it's a nice gesture to give your neighbors a heads-up and drop off a token, like a good bottle of wine or some gourmet goodies, in case the noise level will be higher than usual or if you anticipate having more garbage than usual on your shared curb space. (If you feel weird about acknowledging you are having a party to your neighbors without inviting them to said party, just tell them you're having a work party so they don't feel left out!) There is no normal tipping rate—it's up to you, like in a restaurant. Obviously a larger tip will be met with a larger response, but the range of 5 percent to 20 percent of the final cost of services rendered is most commonly used to measure tip amounts. I can assure you that any tip of any size will be appreciated. If you do forgo tips, I promise you the tip fairy won't report you to the higher-ups and get you in trouble. You can go on living your life as a good person without a scarlet *T* emblazoned on your forehead.

Miscellaneous costs are sometimes the most challenging monsters of party planning. Much like buying a new home and having the $10,000 boiler burst after you just blew every penny on the down payment, things can go wrong, and you must allocate a small amount of your budget for those instances, such as toilets clogging, extra guests showing up unannounced, and angry neighbor gifts. If you are throwing an event in a public space, you may be liable to supply a certificate of **insurance** or get special **permits.** This is where your slush fund comes in handy—just be sure to research these hidden costs beforehand via the Internet or call your local chamber of commerce or city hall to get prices. It is best to squeeze out 3 percent to 5 percent of your budget before even starting to plan your event, put it away, and forget about it. Hopefully this money will just be a pleasant surprise postevent, but it's there if you need it. Try to pay for everything preevent so you are not hit with postevent money meltdown. However, there will always be a few trickles of **fee pee.**

KEEPING AN EYE ON COSTS

Be real careful about paying for your event with credit cards. Racking up frequent flyer miles is a wonderful thing, but racking up finance charges is a whole other ball game. It can be challenging because that swiping motion is so lovely and easy, isn't it? Debit cards are such a wonderful invention, they make me want to cry. I adore their honest, upfront attitude. I love that they wear the credit card Superman costume but have the reliable Clark Kent interior. One can always look on one's online banking site to see where that debit card has been all night.

Keep track of what you are spending with receipts, and keep them in a designated shoebox or folder. Check on your budget as you would an infant in a crib, and make sure it's still breathing and not escaping your grasp. If you know your way around Microsoft Excel, keep an ongoing budget spreadsheet and update it as you buy items or services. If you see an area that is getting out of control and you are OK with that, then you need to decide which of the other areas will be compromised to keep everything on track.

It doesn't matter where ... just keep your receipts! DAVID PFENDLER

If you find that you're way off the mark in terms of your budget, don't panic. You just need to rethink things. Get out your pen and make a list: Under A, write down the things you think your party can't live without; under B, the things you are on the fence about. The A list should include the basics such as food, drinks, and entertainment. Take a look at how extravagant you may have been with any of these items and see if there is any area you can slim down. You don't have to wow your guests *constantly*—save your pennies for one experience that will be memorable—Brazilian drummers marching through the sea of guests or a cool rental for kids like a trampoline or video games. The B list should be fluffy stuff, like parting gifts, guest favors, specialty foods like sushi, **specialty drinks** or champagne (which can easily be substituted with a high-end sparkling wine), and desserts— remember that an overabundance of

More extravagant selections like sushi should go on your "maybe" list. ANDRE MAIER PHOTOGRAPHY

desserts will probably go to waste once guests have had appetizers and dinner, so small bits of sweetness will suffice. If you're having a sit-down dinner, you can serve three instead of five courses to save cash, or serve the dinner buffet style to cut down on waitstaff costs.

To keep entertainment within your budget, you have more options than the obvious iPod playlist on the home stereo scenario. Event professionals tend to charge more, but there are a lot of talented people out there. Scout out new talent

Simple Gloriosa lilies in bud vases are inexpensive and elegant.
ANDRE MAIER PHOTOGRAPHY

at local universities and music schools—most of these young people would love to make a few bucks on the side.

When decorating your space, think large quantities of one thing rather than a bunch of different elements. An event can look very sophisticated glittering with tons of candles that you bought in bulk at a store like Costco or Sam's Club. A mishmash of flowers, candles, and

tschockes tends to look cheaper even if it isn't.

If you want gorgeous flowers at your event and have a limited budget, you are better off designing one amazing arrangement as a centrally located focal point. Use large amounts of one kind of flower. A large vase filled with simple daisies is more visually striking than a bunch of mixed arrangements all over the house or venue.

1. *Edit your guest list:* Take a look your invitees and rethink those guests you could do without. This won't be your last party— you can invite certain people another time.

2. *Change the date:* If you are renting a venue, throw your party on a Friday night or Sunday afternoon rather than paying the much higher-priced rate on Saturday evening. You can also choose seasons that are not as popular: The winter months after the holidays are usually slow times when you can negotiate a better deal.

3. *Keep it short and sweet:* You don't need to party for a hundred hours. The object is to leave your guests wanting more than dying to get out of there.

Simple Things That Look Bling

- Creative lighting is a way to completely transform a space without having to do much. You can change the color of an entire room by using different lightbulbs or by using a gel on recessed lights—and the effect is pretty stunning.

- Mirrors add mega-bling—they open up a space and people adore gazing at themselves when they're feeling sexy and celebratory. You can use wall mirrors, floor mirrors, mirrored vases for florals, or even smaller mirrors as coasters.

Mirrors are the ultimate cheap and easy accent (that looks anything but cheap). WWW.HENSHALLPHOTOGRAPHY.COM

- Use larger, voluptuous flowers that will make a bigger splash rather than lots of little flowers all over the place. Peonies, hydrangeas, sunflowers, and dahlias have a great presence that allows you to use less stems and still fake a bountiful arrangement. A single peony in a small vase is more impressive to me than ten smaller flowers, like freesia, sitting in the same vase.

A mini "Sensation" calla lily added to each napkin is simply sensational. ANDRE MAIER PHOTOGRAPHY

- Provide noticeable details, such as a single flower on each napkin or a nice napkin tie made of wired ribbon or tied grass at a dinner party. I also like a small flower on each passing tray of appetizers. Create cool seating cards for your guests, such as writing the guest's name on a rock—if it's fall, try it on a big colorful leaf from your backyard.

Serve fries in cool colored paper cups to cut costs.
ANDRE MAIER PHOTOGRAPHY

4. *Go disposable:* Use good-quality disposable products rather than renting or buying high-end dinnerware and glassware. If disposable is just too tacky for you, buy real plates but buy smartly at stores like IKEA or Target.

5. *Find The One:* For decorations, pick one thing you adore and go with that. Better yet, find something you can buy in bulk, like votive candles or twinkly lights.

6. *Look beneath the top shelf:* For alcohol, you don't need to buy top of the line. Substitute more affordable Prosecco sparkling wine for champagne, and try out a new vodka that doesn't have a swanky label but might be just as good (if not better) than the famous brand. Ask the staff at your local liquor store to educate you.

7. *Buy in bulk:* Go to a store like Costco or Sam's and embrace those Hormel party platters! Buying more will most likely save you money in the long run.

8. *Find workable spaces:* Choose venues that are party ready—don't choose a place that you need to put tons of cash into for it to be in working order in time for your event. Make sure your power requirements are all there so you don't have to rent a generator.

9. *Go indoors:* The cost of outdoor parties can get out of hand, especially if the **weather** goes awry. All of a sudden, you need tenting, flooring, heating, or air-conditioning. Indoor parties are not vulnerable to these added costs.

10. *Use in-house stuff:* When renting a venue, try to use whatever they have in-house already, like tables, chairs, and linens. If you really can't bear the sight of their house linens, use them as an underlayer and rent a more cost-effective sheer to mask the abomination. If the chairs are

fugly, rent chair covers that will make your tushy proud.

FIVE WAYS TO DO IT YOURSELF

1. *Light:* Change every lightbulb in your house to a new hue. Choose different-toned lightbulbs in your living room, dining room, kitchen, den, and outdoor areas, and make each room stand out in a funky, festive way.

2. *Cook:* Now, I have heard through the grapevine that you can actually turn on an oven and make your own food. Yes, this is allowed—especially for appetizers like mini pizzas, pigs in a blanket, mini quiches, and even huge vats of lasagna. Premaking and freezing will alleviate tons of pressure the day of your event. The same goes for baking: Instead of buying that $18 per slice cake at the patisserie, you can easily bake one yourself or do away with cake altogether

and provide an assortment of fun baked goods like cookies or cookie bars.

3. *Sew*: Are you crafty? Give yourself a thimble manicure and sew your own linens, place mats, furniture covers, pillows, or **floor cushions.** You can even sew cool drapes or room dividers that will give your traditional ranch the cool vibe of a South Beach hotel.

4. *Clean:* Wait until you are in prime PMS mode and take your house to another level of godliness by giving your space the scrubbing of a lifetime—preparty or postparty.

5. *Print:* Thanks to the wonderful Avery company, you can buy printable labels, **postcards,** gift cards, CD labels, and more. Instead of a pricey trip to the stationery store, just make your own invitations, escort cards, and thank-you notes. You can design

them yourself from scratch (after braving a Photoshop lesson—or ten) or work from a template. Or scour the graphic arts design programs at local schools and get a mini pro to help you out!

• • •

Like fiber in your diet, budgets aren't fun, but they're necessary. I say just get the money thing over with as best you can so you can sit back, relax, and host your event worry free.

CHAPTER THREE

The Concept: Your Party's Raison d'Être

You know how it's easier to conquer a hard yoga pose if you keep your eyes on a fixed object in front of you? In much the same way, it's helpful to keep your mind focused on a concept for your event when you are in the planning stages—it keeps your path steady and gives your party definition. But first, let's define *concept.* I use the word concept instead of *theme,* because it's a more diverse and open-ended word; it allows you to be a bit more eclectic, rather than formulaic, when you are conceiving ideas. A concept allows you to say a + b = z, not just the cookie-cutter a + b = c all of the time. If you want a Moroccan theme, you would look up everything Moroccan on the Internet or check out Moroccan travel books, and you'd incorporate that info into your

event, element by element. But if you choose a Moroccan concept, I think you're freer to take Moroccan elements and mix them with your own—still expressing who you are while conveying a Moroccan flavor. I like the freedom of the word because it's not set in stone, whereas the term theme feels like party prison to me.

Having a concept allows your guests to focus on something other than a conversation around the chip-and-dip bowl or on what the other guests are wearing. If you decide to work with a Zen concept at your party, it's fun to watch Joe Schmo from the golf course stare at that six-foot Buddha statue you placed in the living room where your sofa used to be (hey, you can always explain that the sofa was reincarnated). A concept adds dimension to an event

that goes beyond balloons and special party hats. It gives people something to talk about. Concepts are also a great way to introduce a part of you that your friends, family, or coworkers might not know about. If you happen to adore watercolor painting or rockabilly music, you could use these elements as a concept for your party and introduce those around you to an unseen side of you in a creative and interactive way.

Now, you may not think it necessary to come up with an overarching concept for a casual get-together or a small dinner party, but I believe it's always helpful to think up some unifying principle that will tie the evening together, like using a color palette that runs throughout the event. You can create a concept around texture, like velvet,

Floor pillows and a hookah express a Moroccan vibe without going over the top. ANDRE MAIER PHOTOGRAPHY

that can be used in table linens, place mats, pillows, and more. A note about quantities: If you have a thing for orchids, go ahead and choose orchids as your concept, but you don't have to have orchids overflowing from every nook and cranny in the space. There should just be enough to make a noticeable orchid stamp on the room by using them in centerpieces, as an accent on passing trays, folded in napkins, or if you are having a focal piece such as a cake, they could make an appearance there.

Color Your World

When organizing a principle around a color palette, don't use exact same colors but combinations that complement and harmonize with each other. Some of my favorite color combos are orange and brown, hot pink and orange, deep violet and chartreuse green, ivory and white, copper and ivory, and chocolate brown and many colors like French blue, lavender, pink, and yellow. (Brown is a great base color that is not as severe as black but has a richness to it that bears a nice weight that can hold down lighter colors.) For saturated hues, I adore navy blue and black, navy blue and lavender, and jewel tones like amethyst, ruby, emerald, and sapphire.

These brightly colored bouquets show off some of my favorite color combos. ANDRE MAIER PHOTOGRAPHY

Love orchids? Use your concept sparingly. ANDRE MAIER PHOTOGRAPHY

In fact, it's smart to place your conceptual elements in focal points of the room, like on a dinner table or (believe it or not) in the bathroom where the focus is pretty easy to manipulate. Your concept will affect how the guests feel upon entering the room. Through the party's concept and ambience, you want to evoke an emotional response from your guests—hopefully a good one!

(For a more detailed discussion on party ambience, see chapter 6.) But overall, don't let the concept define you—you define the concept and control how much or how little you'd like to express it.

LET'S CONCEPTUALIZE!

To define your own party concept, the first thing you need to do is take a long, hard look at the reason you are celebrating. If it's a birthday party for a three-year-old boy—before even thinking about spewing the color blue from every pore in your house—think about the boy himself. Does he love music? Dinosaurs? Cheerios? What is a consistent common denominator in this kid's life (stepping aside from the obvious branded themes of *Thomas the Train* and *Go, Diego, Go!)*? For instance, my nephew Solomon adores wearing stripes. If I were to have a party for him, my concept would be to have stripes everywhere: **faux striped wallpaper,** striped linens, striped napkins in

crazy colors, striped invitations, striped balloons, striped beanbag chairs, and even a striped cake! Go to the next level and ask yourself what else has stripes that toddlers would like? Throw some life-size inflatable zebras into the mix. In a short time, you've created a cool concept for this party that expresses who this guy is in a unique way to his family and friends.

Another rule of thumb: Choose concepts that are achievable. You may want to re-create the Sahara in your living room, but before you dump a thousand pounds of sand and camel poop on your carpet, think *smaller.* A more doable option might be to express the desert motif through hues: Create a **monochromatic color scheme** using a palette that spans from light sandy brown all the way to deeper chocolate tones, adding hints of oasis colors like cerulean blue or leafy green. You can do this by covering your existing furniture in **flame-retardant fabric** in neutral

Stripe it rich for a kid's party that goes beyond the cookie-cutter mold.
DAVID PFENDLER

colors and then adding a pop of oasis in the form of pillows, **floor cushions,** drapes, colored glass, candles, and more.

You can also make your point a bit more literally by using some cool camel and palm tree silhouettes on the wall with cutout **vinyl decals, stencils,** or lighting patterns made out of **gobos.** Take some patterned fabric (or even bed sheets) and create some makeshift bedouin tents tied to existing furniture inside your home, between trees, or to staked poles (such as broom handles) in your backyard. Furnish the forts with floor matting, fabric-covered milk crates with cushioned tops, and a low, flat-topped surface for food and drinks, which can easily be one of your own coffee tables draped with fabric. If you are really feeling the desert vibe, you can even put a small wading pool smack dab in the middle of your party—a virtual oasis! Put a heavy drop cloth on the floor first, and place a smaller pool within a bigger one. Make a sandy or green foliage "moat" in the larger pool, pour water in the smaller pool, and float some gorgeous tropical leaves or water lilies and floating candles on top.

It's possible to have a great event without doing much to your space physically, but I think one always need to add some sort of **wow factor,** just to keep your guests breathing. These elements can be small, like perhaps serving a **specialty drink** in a vibrant color (like a blood orange cosmo) or providing party buckets filled with ice and mini beers and champagne bottles; serve colorful straws alongside these baby bottles, and the guests can help themselves. Display snacks throughout the house on **tiered platters** and offer Mini-Me versions of favorite foods, such as tiny club sandwiches or bite-size pizzas. These are all simple, easy ways to increase the wow factor of a get-together.

Another way to add punch to your party is to offer some sort of interactive play for your guests. This can run the gamut from a mixed-up seating chart at a dinner party (encouraging mingling where it would normally not occur) all the way to games and scavenger hunts. One time, my fella and I threw a cocktail party in our home because we missed our friends. We didn't want it to be boring and we wanted to make sure everyone was entertained since many of the guests didn't know each other. Our first ideas included a mechanical bull

This party's concept was "Nights over Egypt"—hence the sphinx.
ANDRE MAIER PHOTOGRAPHY

Playing the game at a bat mitzvah.
ANDRE MAIER PHOTOGRAPHY

or naked Twister, but we settled upon renting a fabulous Japanese video game called *Dance Dance Revolution*. People went crazy for this game! Mind you, the average age of the guests attending our event was one hundred and fifty, so we were surprised and thrilled by its popularity. By having this machine set up in our backyard, we were able to relax about the fact that we didn't have catering or that we limited the bar—because the game gave us that extra fun push that got the guests talking and moving. It was also quite entertaining to watch our friends get on this ridiculous machine where all social inhibitions seemed to fade away. Our guests still talk about our run-of-the-mill cocktail party because of that game. But proceed with caution when planning interactive activities, because you don't want your event to become segregated or overly gregarious in one area and a complete dud in another. Think about who you are inviting and choose activities that are conducive to bringing the guests together—not keeping them apart.

I am not a huge fan of asking guests to wear a certain color to an event, but suggesting attire can make a party more conceptual. Attire can span from casual chic to black tie. Why do this? If you are throwing a barbecue in your backyard, I would assume your guests would rather not be told what to wear, so it's not always appropriate. But even though the idea may seem stuffy and outmoded to some, when you provide attire direction, it helps guests comprehend the type of event they will be attending. In addition, the timing can dictate the feel of the party. If the event is held during the day, we girls tend to not get tarted up with tons of makeup and glitter powder in our cleavage. If the event falls within the hours of an average cocktail party (say, 7:00 p.m. to 9:00 p.m.) then we know it's OK to wear those $200 jeans with a cute sexy top and some fab dangly things on our ears. The time frame of the event helps people decide what to wear so some of the attire responsibilities are already taken care of.

I've included a bunch of ideas to get your creative juices flowing. Always know that you can simply pump up the volume on your current environment in lieu of an organized concept. You can bling out your living room by adding candles, colored lightbulbs, pillows, music . . . and cleaning it would be good too!

CELEBRATE AN ANNIVERSARY

Have a **brunch!** People really dig breakfasty food. Consider brioche French toast marinated in Jack Daniels and butter, or perhaps a chorizo, onion, and blue cheese frittata and homemade smoothies. Try mimosas with other types of alcohol, like tequila or sake, and other juices like sparkling blueberry juice.

    Outdoor parties are great for laid-back, casual fun. Provide your guests with individual picnic baskets and plush seats on the ground in a park or at the beach. Since blankets are not sturdy enough to create comfortable seating, set up large ultrasuede **floor cushions,** low cube ottomans, or even old school beanbag chairs on shag rugs.

When designating attire for your party, make it more interesting than "Business Casual"—call it "Bohemian Chic." DAVID PFENDLER

Have a professional chef give an **in-home cooking class** for you and a few friends. The couples drink wine and socialize while they learn to cook a decadent meal. This type of event can be held in a private home or even a rented loft with a kitchen.

    Travel back to your dating days and hold a **roller-skating** or **bowling party.** Or **rent a drive-in** movie

Specialty drinks, like this passion fruit tequila sunrise, add panache.
ANDRE MAIER PHOTOGRAPHY

theater and provide gourmet grown-up movie treats, like homemade ice cream sandwiches, spiced popcorn, and rum-infused milkshakes. You can even hold a retro mixer in the local gym or rec hall with cool paper streamer decor and disco ball lights. Don't forget to spike the punch bowl!

SHAKE UP THE BRIDAL SHOWER

Put a twist on the average spa day by starting off with a group **pole-dancing class** (mothers and mothers-in-law included for extra points)! After working up a sweat, get your spa treatments on and chow down on some sugared-up spa treats like caramel yogurt, maple-infused granola, fresh berries dipped in dark chocolate, and (of course) peach Bellinis.

Show some **flower power**—enlist the wedding florist to take the bride and her crew to the local flower market for a behind-the-scenes tour and an in-depth class on how to make the ultimate arrangement. After all that learning, treat the posse to hot stone mani/pedis while sipping on ginger beer and green tea cocktails.

Invite an **oral historian** to interview the favorite women in the bride's life on the subject of love. Enjoy a lazy lunch while friends, mothers, and grandmothers weave a beautiful tapestry of talk—something the bride can have in her possession for a lifetime. Serve an assortment of aromatic teas, scones, finger sandwiches, cookies, and mint juleps.

Throw the **slumber party** of a lifetime for the bride and her girls—no boys allowed! Serve homemade gourmet pizzas family style; after bellies are full and the presents have been opened, retire to the den to watch chick flicks while snacking on spicy popcorn and Rice Krispie treats. If you feel like splurging, it's cute to offer matching robes and fuzzy slippers before they climb onto their air mattress for the night.

GO FOR BIRTHDAY BLOWOUTS

Road trip! None of us want our birthdays to last only one day, so take it on the road with some of your favorite friends. Rent an Airstream or Winnebago and map out a realistic course, like Los Angeles to Vegas or New York to Vermont. Hit all the star attractions, pack some gourmet goodies to go (such as wrap sandwiches with filet mignon, horseradish mustard, and grilled onions coupled with thick-cut potato chips). When you've reached your destination (and stopped driving), hit the local scene and make them remember you!

Rent a cabin somewhere fabulous and invite your guests to take a moon-light hike or horse ride through nature. Open your presents around a campfire complete with spiked cider and hot chocolate and snacks like old-school hot dogs and s'mores.

The stars will always be older than you, so take your celebration to the **planetarium.** Sip on champagne while you travel through the heavenly skies; once the laser light show gets going, pump up the disco and bring in another year having a celestial blast.

Work up an appetite with a night out at a local **salsa club.** You and your friends can give your hips a proper workout while watching the real pros take it away. There should be margaritas and mojitos for everyone!

THIS ONE IS JUST FOR THE HELL OF IT!

Sometimes a girl just needs a reason to put her tits on and be festive. You've been working hard, cleaning house, and entertaining your kids. Take a stab at happiness and celebrate for no particular reason!

Throw a **board game party** at the park with a plethora of retro games like Othello, Connect Four, and Battleship. Be careful to bring games that are wind friendly so you won't be chasing after game pieces. To stoke the competitive fires, hand out individual lunch boxes (if you want to go all out, buy some retro ones from eBay that befit your generation) containing schoolyard favorites like peanut butter and Marshmallow Fluff sandwiches (if you really love your friends, add some banana slices, honey, or chocolate syrup into the mix), yogurt-covered pretzels, homemade fruit roll-ups, and, in lieu of a juice box, spice up the afternoon with thermoses filled with spiked fruit juice. For those who want to keep their heads clear so they can sink your battleship, offer vanilla or chocolate soy milk. Pin several picnic blankets together to create a Technicolor dream blanket that tons of friends can relax on together. Cool plastic trays from Target or IKEA will create a nice firm surface to prevent spillage and support the more serious gamers in your crowd.

The **house party** is one of my faves and is very easy to produce. Keep it simple with a barbecue or make some cholesterol-laden favorites like fried chicken and ribs with sumptuous sides of mac and cheese, Tater Tots, and French fries

Lots of beer is a must at a house party. JES GORDON

sangria with a hit of sparkling wine to give it some gas. Scatter colorful plastic snack bowls around the house filled with popcorn sprinkled with garlic salt or chili pepper. Stack up a plate filled with sweets that could survive a nuclear holocaust: Twinkies, Ring Dings, Funny Bones, and Sno Balls. Or, if you're feeling ambitious, you could bake **cupcakes** yourself—since you never know how old those Twinkies are.

CHILD'S PLAY

Kids are much more like grown-ups than we give them credit for—they're just smaller and more honest. Kids vary in their personalities and predilections, just like adults do.

That said, certain fail-safe things can make kids happy, such as candy, games, colors, sounds, and security. I say security because kids want to feel safe and surrounded. So when throwing the ultimate kids' party, don't only think about tiring them out—think about making them feel secure, entertained, and most of all, included.

coupled with some good old Heinz or glammed up with some truffle oil or curried mayonnaise. Make your own picnic tables out of simple four-by-eight plywood boards on top of sawhorses found at any Home Depot or hardware store. House parties

always feature a keg of beer or some sort of insane punch in the kitchen. Give this a modern, grown-up spin by supplying a beer bar made from several mini-size kegs of imported beer sitting in a long trough filled with ice; instead of jungle juice, serve white

Kids need love, attention . . . and cake. ANDRE MAIER PHOTOGRAPHY

For the ultimate **pillow party,** move everything out of a room by stashing loose objects in a hall closet, pushing large pieces of furniture aside, and padding all surfaces and floors with pillows. Use double-sided Velcro to stick pillows onto surfaces—just be sure to use gaffing tape on furniture or walls to protect them from the double-sided products. Use oversize floor pillows for seating for adult guardians (and for kids to flop on).

Make multicolored pillow cases by quick stitching fabric together, or just buy pillow cases with fun themes on them—superheroes, dolls, or whatever the fads are. Send out pillow cases as invitations, decorated with those laundry-friendly fabric pens or paints from any art supply or hobby store. If you're feeling campy, you can order iron-on letters on the Internet. The guests can draw and write messages on plain pillow cases with fabric marker so

they have a cool camplike keepsake to bring home. A good snack to fit with the pillow concept is a simple sheet cake cushioned with tons of marshmallows. Keep the cushiony texture going with individual angel food or sponge cakes, Mallomars, and Rice Krispie treats. And obviously, the party game is . . . a pillow fight!

A **dance party** is all about music and boogying down. You should provide a **dance floor** where the little peeps won't feel too much in the spotlight and get too self-conscious to participate. Make this area darker than the rest of the room by turning off the overhead lights or equipping them with a bulb in deep red, orange, or pink—or all three! If you don't feel like purchasing a disco ball, you can buy lightbulbs that have reflective surfaces or ripples in their glass that cast a cool reflection onto the direct surface they are closest to, creating that disco vibe. Provide some current **playlists** on your iPod and have groups of kids play DJ for the event.

The dimly lit dance floor at a Sweet Sixteen party. ANDRE MAIER PHOTOGRAPHY

Go cruise Radio Shack or Best Buy and get a karaoke machine—prices vary from $19.99 to a couple of hundred for ones that come with lighting and computer graphics.

All kids are budding Picassos, so throw them an **inner artiste party.** Invitations should definitely be made out of some original art! If your kid's little hands don't feel

up to hand making every invitation, just scan in a recent work for the cover and get it printed at Kinko's or through Internet-based shops like VistaPrint or MOO. At the event, provide a low table with tons of art supplies—paper, crayons, markers, paint (all washable, of course), clay, glue, glitter, stickers, and more. (Depending on the age group, I would avoid the whole scissors thing—you do the math on that one.) Give guests an easy-to-use digital camera and let the kids take pics of themselves. Print out the photos while the kids are still there, pin them on a corkboard, and let them collect their images at the end of the party. The guests could also make photo collages to keep or give away to their BFFs. Handing out simple white T-shirts that the kids can draw on with fabric pens is another great art idea—and it doubles as the party favor. Regarding nibbles, it's hard to take a break from the creative process—especially if your hands are covered in paint—so it would be cool if each artist had his or her own apron complete with pockets. Tuck healthy, easy-to-grab snacks in the apron pockets, like nuts, yogurt-covered raisins and pretzels, carrot sticks, and cheese sticks. When your artists are ready to take a break for some real substance, offer a visual feast of food such as bowls of gorgeous fruit, baskets of bread, and luscious fondue pots filled with rich chocolate or cheese. With fondue, the artists can continue getting their hands dirty!

Hell, just give in to their whining demands once a year and have a **sweets for the sweet party** with no healthy food. Set up an ice-cream sundae bar with frozen yogurt or ice cream and a complete selection of candy and fruit toppings. Kids can go to different decorating stations where they can top cookies or cupcakes with frosting and sprinkles. On the floor, replicate a huge Candyland game board on a white plastic tarp either by drawing it yourself with nonsmearing art markers or having the artwork printed on vinyl at a print shop—not only does this protect your floor, it keeps the

You can rent a special candy machine to match your party colors. ANDRE MAIER PHOTOGRAPHY

concept in mind. I also love a candy bar (in fact, I have one in my home on a permanent basis). Construct your own candy landscape by using old mason jars or simple discount-store glass vases of all different shapes and sizes; filled with assortments of candy, they'll look like a colorful skyline. Next to each jar of candy, put a guessing jar so each guest can guess the number of candies inside on slips of paper. The winner gets . . . more candy! Or have a silly recipe contest, where you hand out simple recipe cards for something common like chocolate chip cookies—but you leave out one ingredient, Mad Libs style (à la "sugar, flour, eggs, butter, and _____"). Trust me, the responses will be hilarious. Make sure you have your guests sign their pieces of paper so you can read them aloud and crack everybody up!

SOME NEW IDEAS FOR THE HOLIDAYS

Bah, humbug, yo. When I think about holiday parties, I think about weight gain, family drama, and stress. Holiday entertaining usually

Decking the halls for the holidays.
ANDRE MAIER PHOTOGRAPHY

goes something like this: When you finally get to sit down and enjoy your family, you are too exhausted to even care. Holidays shouldn't be like this—so here are some quick ideas to alleviate this *mishegas.*

With the **conceptual potluck party** there is nothing tacky about asking guests to bring something—you're not skimping, you're simply encouraging others to share in the creation of this event! (And you're saving yourself some precious sanity in the process.) So tell folks to bring something other than the ubiquitous green bean casserole—get them involved in the environment as well. Let's call it a creative co-op. As with any type of cooperative effort, it's helpful to have a solid structure to work within, so I suggest coming up with a holiday palette for the party. Instead of regular red and green and blue and white, reimagine your own holiday hues like chocolate brown and copper—or put a spin on the originals by using navy blue and silver for a Hanukkah party. This way, when you request potluck items, such as cupcakes, desserts, candles, table linens, platters, flowers, or drinks, you can tell guests to keep the color palette in mind when they make their offering. It's much more interesting to see how it all comes together with a group effort.

If you need a change of scenery, create an **all around the world party** that mirrors a holiday in a different region. Research how people celebrate in other countries like France, China, or somewhere that resonates for you personally. In Sweden a lovely tradition on December 13th (said to be the longest night of the year) features a young girl dressed as Saint Lucia in a white gown with a crown of candles and greenery in her hair bringing a tray of sweets to the guests. In Costa Rica at Christmas people decorate their homes with bright tropical flowers and fresh fruit. The older generation in your family may be a wonderful source for this type of get-together. Mine them for inspiration, and make cool ornaments out of old family photos. Make photocopies of treasured pics, cut out scenes, and glue them onto a simple glass ornament with adhesive spray. For a shiny finish, spray the ornament with hair spray or a clear coat of artist varnish. Hang antique items like baby booties and jewelry from the tree; slip meaningful trinkets like foreign currency or old letters into clear glass ornaments. For the holiday meal, clear out some space in your family room to create an intimate "dinner in the round" at a round table or just on the floor. Sitting in the round is more conducive for storytelling and allows us to speak freely. Lazy Susans are one of my favorite

This Christmas party featured tables wrapped up like gifts.
ANDREW BICKNELL PHOTOGRAPHY

things—let the feast tour the table, family style. If you need to sit on the floor, make sure you provide soft seating surfaces and individual trays for guests. You can easily balance more worldly elements with more traditional ones so you don't freak out your family with too much of the unexpected. Keep the old favorites like a tree or a menorah but also offer different types of food like dim sum or pita and hummus!

The aesthetic for a **rockin' around the Christmas tree party** should be retro Americana, ripped from the set of *Mad Men*—bedeck your halls with mid-century touches like vintage bubble Christmas tree lights, a shiny tinsel tree, and strong, old-fashioned cocktails like gin martinis and Manhattans. Serve classic party fare, like pigs in a blanket (but upgraded with spicy chorizo and carmelized onions in a puff pastry dough, served with a mustard dipping sauce), deviled eggs made with crème fraîche instead of mayo and topped with caviar, and champagne gelatin treats with fresh berries. The hi-fi can play a mix of holiday tunes from the era to get people in the swinging mood.

If you live in a cold climate, a **dashing through the snow party** is a perfect December get-together. Gather a group to go cross-country skiing, have a snowball fight, or a snowman-making contest—or if you're not into working up a sweat at parties, arrange a lovely sleigh ride pulled by Clydesdale horses, straight out of a Budweiser commercial. For the people who want to stay inside, create a cozy lounging space around the fireplace with overstuffed chairs, floor pillows, and personalized fleece throws for everyone (get cheap ones at Bed Bath & Beyond and make them special with iron-on monograms). Warm up your guests with steaming hot toddies, spiked cocoa, and dunkable desserts like spicy ginger thins and anise biscotti. For heartier tummies, serve an easy slow-cooker dish like beef bourguignon, paired with crusty rosemary olive bread. Table decorations should evoke the great outdoors, with pinecones, boughs of greenery, twigs, and warm white candlelight. Enlist your kids to make cutout snowflakes you can hang from fishing line from the ceiling—or channel your own inner child and make them yourself! Decorating with ice is twice as nice: Buy silicone ice-cube trays in fun shapes, like reindeer, stars, or penguins, and serve the cubes in your specialty drink, or feature an ice sculpture of a snowman as your party's wow factor.

● ● ●

If you are still completely at a loss about your party concept, think once again: What is the reason for your event and who are you inviting? Churning this constantly through your mind will help steer you away from tacky themes and boring styles. And you can never go wrong organizing an event around a color palette or flower if you want to keep it simple.

CHAPTER FOUR

Location, Location, Location: Where to Party?

A direct sight line to the ocean made this location extraordinary.
WWW.HENSHALLPHOTOGRAPHY.COM

I've thrown parties everywhere imaginable: trailer parks, bathrooms, conference rooms, basements, backyards, hallways—you name it. And what I've learned from these radically different spaces is that

one's choice in venue can determine *everything* about your party. That choice can be as simple as deciding whether you want to have a modern space or an old-world glam one. If you like to be in control, you may

want to choose a blank-slate venue—like an all-white photo studio or warehouse space where you can orchestrate the environment. If you've always fantasized about some enchanted evening straight out of a Disney fairy tale, you can rent a venue that looks like a castle! Overall, venues should help express what's important to you as a host—whether it's a city skyline, cozy seating, or just plenty of restrooms. The venue does more than set the stage for your party—it is the stage.

HOUSE PARTIES

Most people think that having a party at home is best—less costly, less fuss, that sort of thing—which is probably true as long as you are aware that there are many things you need to do in order to make a

Making use of the mantel at a house party. JES GORDON

home party ready. After all, giving your home up to the party gods is easier said than done. Your home is your private sanctuary and though you may want to share it with friends and family, even the most gracious

hosts among us are unnerved to see someone spilling red wine all over their carpet, or catching that weird friend-of-a-friend going through your underwear drawer. If you decide to entertain in your home, here are some precautions you can take to avoid having to spend the next month in a Motel 6.

1. Stash away the good stuff. Closet your most valued items, like **antiques/artwork,** cash, fancy jewelry, and fragile knickknacks—really, anything important to you. You can even go the Pink Panther route and buy a cool safe from Costco or Staples and lock it up.

2. Get your home ready to take on the world of party messiness by applying **Scotchgard** to furniture and fabrics, like sofas, chairs, curtains, and rugs. If you are fabulous enough to own some very expensive pieces, you may want to consider storing

those items in your garage or spare room and replacing them with less-expensive versions, like a faux Oriental rug from Bed, Bath & Beyond. Or simply cover your existing furniture with temporary slipcovers.

3. People love hanging out in the kitchen at parties (even though this can be very annoying to those who are actually using this room for practical purposes), so make sure the kitchen is socialized: Constantly clean up any food prep work, and be sure to not leave any surface burners on. Turn your kitchen into a clean, well-oiled machine, and enlist your partner, kids, or whomever to make that happen.

4. Prepare your guest bathroom(s) for the night of its life by providing lots of toilet paper, hand towels, hand soap, lotion, breath mints, **air freshener** or matches, Tums or Rolaids,

This bathroom is ready for action. ANDREW BICKNELL PHOTOGRAPHY

the police, which can really kill the vibe. Your guests are your responsibility when they are in your home, so if you see anyone acting more like a nutcase than usual, take notice and figure out what the deal is. If a guest has had too much to drink, it's your duty to play bad cop and cut the offender off. It's an awkward situation to be sure, but you don't want someone you know slipping into a coma on your kitchen floor either.

hairbrush, aspirin, menstrual products, and a turbo toilet plunger, ever ready for disaster. That said, it's also a good idea to have a toilet brush and cleaner on hand as well.

5. If you are having a large number of guests and you don't feel your number of bathrooms will fit the bill, don't be afraid to go the **Porta-Potty** route. They have come a long way since construction site johns.

6. Safety is key, so be sure you have good-citizen items on hand, such as fire extinguishers (one for every room), a first-aid kit, usable phones in case of a power outage, and a cab company on call for inebriated guests. Stay focused on the noise level so you won't attract the attention of

7. Parents, put your kids away for the night. Seeing your parents (or your parents' friends) blitzed out of their minds is a surefire road to therapy. It's cool to have kids say hello to your guests at the beginning of the event, but it's best to create a safe space for them upstairs or in a basement playroom that is off limits to your guests. Equip the room with engrossing

Believe it or not, this is a toilet. ANDRE MAIER PHOTOGRAPHY

eating. Guests won't want to be cut off from the music outside, and wiring up some temporary speakers is simply done. Either move some speakers outside for the party, or scout out some outdoor-friendly ones at places like Best Buy. (Just be sure to tape up any running wires so guests don't trip.) You also want to make sure there is enough **outdoor lighting** so your guests can see each other.

entertainment—favorite DVDs, video games, and food that will likely rot their teeth. If you have little ones, hire their favorite babysitter to keep them occupied for the evening.

8. When the **weather** is pleasant, any outdoor space should be attended to as well. Make sure your **lawn** and shrubbery are manicured so that your guests don't have to use weed whackers in order to mingle. Cover up bald spots on the lawn with high-quality **AstroTurf.** Pluck all dog poop from the lawn, turn off your sprinklers a few days before your party so your yard doesn't become a Woodstockian mud pit, get on bug patrol with **citronella candles** and fly traps, provide **ashtrays** and plenty of friendly surfaces for sitting and

9. Then take a chill pill. If you are going to spend the entire event playing mess police and telling people they can't behave naturally, then don't put yourself (and the partygoers) through the trauma. You don't want to look back on your event and remember yourself on your knees with seltzer water and salt rubbing imaginary stains out of your shag rug, so relax—or put some cash toward securing a venue.

RENTING A SPACE

The decision to rent a venue is a tough one because obviously it's an added expense, but sometimes when you add up what it will cost to make your home party ready, it could be a wash. Often venues come with in-house catering, tables, chairs, plates, china, glassware, sound systems, and lighting systems—all major items needed to throw an event—so it can actually be more cost-effective to have your celebration under a venue's roof. Venues are also professionally insured, they hold fire **permits,** and have dedicated fire exits and extinguishers placed around the room, so the boring icky stuff is handled by them—not you. Space is another huge deciding factor. You may have an awesome sprawling abode in everyday life, but at a party, your home can shrink to dollhouse proportions.

Guests should have at least four feet dedicated to each of them for a sit-down dinner and at least six to eight feet per person on the dance

This magnificent venue has space to spare. ANDREW BICKNELL PHOTOGRAPHY

floor. You also have to take into account any support staff who need room too—include extra space for these guys. (This equation holds true for venues too; ask the venue manager what the maximum legal capacity is, and don't exceed that capacity.) The venue versus home decision has different pros and cons for every client—it's great to sit back and let a venue take the beating of a party, but if you're a control freak, you may get frustrated. My advice? If you don't have a home large enough to throw the event of your dreams, then mix up a Xanax cocktail, write a check, and let the venue handle the rest.

Your choice of venue should excite you, but don't worry if it

We softened up the hard edges of this loft with lofty pillows.
ANDRE MAIER PHOTOGRAPHY

doesn't have the exact details you imagined. With the proper decor, you can rock out any space with lighting, candles, flowers, fabric, and just happy party people. If you're working with a smaller budget, you may want to consider venues that have in-house amenities, such as tables, chairs, basic lighting, and a caterer. Hotels fall into this category, and they work well since there are so many different types to suit almost any style. If you have a larger budget, consider other venues like lofts, cool old warehouse spaces, or even a recreation center or gymnasium, but remember that in raw spaces, you will need to provide many things yourself. Therefore, allow a space in your budget to bring in tables, chairs, linens, a dance floor, coat-racks, kitchen equipment, staging, lighting, dressing areas, and possibly much more. You may have always wanted to have your event in a castle, but if this castle doesn't have a kitchen, it might not work!

Having to put up an exterior kitchen tent alongside the venue rental itself could put you into a budget tailspin. This is one of many, many scenarios. Overall, you want to pick a place whose staff has experience with the event world and knows the lingo. For instance, managers who know to put fresh toilet paper in the bathroom and facilities that have all the important amenities, like a kitchen, handicapped access, dressing areas, parking or valet capabilities, electricity, air-conditioning in the summer and heating in the winter, and a captain or in-house event coordinator who can act as a point person for your needs.

Pick an age-appropriate venue too. You don't want Grandma or your boss having to slide down a fireman's pole to get to the dinner after the cocktail hour. Choose a

Beware of extra plating charges with outside vendors at venues.
ANDRE MAIER PHOTOGRAPHY

place that has a good floor plan and is conducive to an easy flow of traffic without a lot of bottlenecking.

Find out whether the venue owners will insist upon your using their "preferred" vendors. You may be presented with a select list of florists, caterers, entertainers, and the like; if you don't like their vendors, ask them if they will allow you to bring in your people at no additional cost. However, this will probably incur a charge. Venue owners want to make a profit and will ask you to pay a **plating charge** for an outside cake, or a **corkage fee** for outside alcohol.

Pay attention to the acoustics. If you are talking comfortably in the room and your voices are bouncing off the walls, then brace yourself for added sound engineer costs. Sound engineers usually come with your entertainment package; a band or DJ will most likely bring along a sound engineer who makes sure the band instruments are in tune and at the right sound levels. After all, when your guests are eating dinner and making conversation, your band's rendition of "Pour Some Sugar on Me" should be played at a bearable level. Also, if there are microphone needs for **toasts** or, heaven help us, karaoke, a sound engineer will handle that. If a sound engineer isn't available, you can do a few things to help out in a rotten acoustic situation. The best thing is to strategically place multiple speakers around the entire space that you can switch between during different times of the event. Along with multiple speakers, **monitor speakers** should be placed in front of the band or DJ so the DJ and musicians can hear themselves over the other noise. Venues that have carpeted areas tend to have better acoustics because carpets can aid in buffering and absorbing sound better than a hardwood or concrete floor. If your venue is putting on many events at one time, make sure you won't be able to hear the twenty-five piece drumming circle from the next ballroom at your event; have the venue manager prove to you that the walls or **air wall** that separates the rooms does not let in any air or noise from the other room. Simply ask the person: "Does this wall really do the trick? And is it possible for us to come and see for ourselves during another event?" But if you are

In a multiroomed ballroom venue, air walls can keep stray noise at bay.
DAVID PFENDLER

not having a Buddhist meditation party and are having some form of entertainment, that, in addition to the air wall, will drown out the sound from other rooms. Also ask if any in-house lighting, like pin spotting, which highlights your table centerpieces, will be provided along with spotlights for any presentations. Having those ready to go at a venue can really save time and money down the road.

Airflow is another very important aspect of choosing a location. I don't care if you are having an outdoor brunch in the country, a party at a three-hundred-year-old cathedral, or a picnic at the beach—air movement is crucial. Important questions to ask your venue contact about airflow are:

1. Is there central air-conditioning and heating? If so, how loud is the system? Can you listen to the system to find out if you need to hire a screaming punk band to cover the noise?

2. Is there an extra cost to use in-house heating and cooling?

3. When does the system get turned on for the event? Meaning if the event starts at 7:00 p.m., what time does the air start running? Your venue needs to be comfortable when your guests arrive, and, hopefully, your flower and cake deliveries from earlier in the day have not turned to mush.

4. If the venue does not have a cooling or heating system, ask what is used in place of it. Do huge windows supply a wonderful cross breeze? Are there outdoor heaters for patio areas if the event is held during a colder season? And is it possible to come back to the venue during a colder or warmer month to be sure your party will take place at the desired temperature?

Hand fans will do the trick in a pinch (and they can double as favors).
ANDRE MAIER PHOTOGRAPHY

Rent movable air-conditioning and heating units to be placed in tents. Do not try to get away with renting huge industrial fans for $50 less; they will just blow the wig off Grandpa, as well as blow out the six thousand candles the caterer just lit. Even though it may feel breezy and cool outside, the inside of a tent or venue has a huge amount of wattage running through it from hot lights, the band, the kitchen—not to mention the large group of people dancing their asses off. Keep this in mind also during cold weather: The same wattage/lighting you are using will help you heat the place, so don't turn it into an oven. It's so sad to see photos of people having a good time with sweaty hair plastered to their heads. If you don't have a planner, you need to speak with your in-house contact and make that person aware of this concern. I would bet

Check if the venue has insurance for its stairwells and alternate access for the disabled.
ANDRE MAIER PHOTOGRAPHY

my boobs the venue has gotten air control down to a science by the time you come along, but make sure that that someone is on site to monitor this issue throughout your entire event.

Find out what the maximum capacity for the space is. If you are inviting three hundred people and the venue can only legally house two hundred and fifty guests, that can be very bad. The maximum occupancy is usually listed on a certificate that must be displayed somewhere in the venue by law. This certificate usually hangs near the bar or at the entrance. This is part of the venue's fire code, which is another important thing to inquire about. What are their rules on candlelight? Can we have fire-eaters as entertainers if we want? If a fire marshal decides to do a routine inspection (which can be done at any time), the marshal legally has the right to close down any party if the rules are not being followed, so this is important to nail down preparty. Fire codes may necessitate a certificate of fire-retardant fabric too. If you purchase fire-retardant fabric from a fabric vendor, the purchase should come with a certificate stating that the fabric has been legally treated. If you choose to employ a specialist who can treat any fabric you buy, that person must also provide you with a legal certificate that states that the fabric has been treated. If, sadly, a fire does occur and the fabric does not resist fire in any way, having this certificate makes the provider liable, not you.

SIGNING ON THE DOTTED LINE

If you are ready to take the plunge and rent, remember that venues come with contracts and price tags that you will need to negotiate. Here are some important hints on how to play with the big boys. Before you sign any contracts, make sure that the space is insured against injury and that its contract is solid. The space itself should have **insurance** that would protect you if one of your guests slips and falls on the stairwell, or if the bathroom floor is wet and someone gets injured.

Will the venue be more expensive in another season? ANDRE MAIER PHOTOGRAPHY

It is a sad fact of life that people sue people. I have even seen guests try to sue the hosts of an event they attended after something happens to them because of their own clumsiness! The venue should carry insurance that protects them and you if they suffer from a fire or another act of destruction before or during your event. Don't take any of this stuff personally, and don't freak out. Life is life, and you're better off being prepared for it. Personally, I recommend not signing a contract until a professional event planner or a lawyer friend has combed though it. But if you're on your own, try to collect several contracts from different locations so you can compare to see what makes the most sense and protects you most as the client. Figure out exactly what the contract terms include. If the venue only allows you six hours in the space but the florist needs six hours to set up, you will be going into massive overtime and budget blizzards. Does the contract specify extra charges, such as cleaning fees, freight elevator usage, **electricity drops,** security, parking, coat check, and dressing rooms? Be aware of the payment schedule that the venue lists in its contract. It is normal to pay a deposit to hold the date of your event; the venue is not allowed to give that date away to another client once that deposit is received. It is also common to pay for the venue in full beforehand, so don't be alarmed if the contract states that the final payment is due before your party.

Has the venue been in business for a while, and does it look like

What could be better than cocktails on a rooftop in Manhattan? ANDRE MAIER PHOTOGRAPHY

it's going to stick around? This is a harsh reality, especially in larger cities where venues open and close quickly, sometimes before your event. Therefore, you need to always have a plan B stipulated in your contract. If they (God forbid) go out of business before your party date, they need to provide you with a replacement venue that is of equal or superior quality to your first choice. On the flip side, it's important to

ask venue managers (and all other vendors too) if their prices will be going up if your event is occurring in another season or year. I learned this lesson the hard way when planning my own wedding; our party was in 2009 but we booked our hotel in 2008. Our final bill was higher than we originally budgeted for, because the rates changed.

On a depressing side note: Say your venue reneges on your

contract in some way. You can always negotiate postevent; legally speaking, you have a few months to dispute any items that may come up afterward. If this happens, it's best to go on with the show as best you can. Most of the time your guests will have no idea that something went wrong behind the scenes, so try not to throw a shit fit. Once your event is over, don't rush out and hire a lawyer; request a meeting with the venue management to discuss the issues at hand. This is why having a rock-solid, detailed contract is so important—it makes it hard for the venue staff to later insist that they thought you said pink linens when you really said blue. If those negotiations don't work out, go ahead and take your issues to *Judge Judy* after you have thought long and hard about it.

When booking your venue, be budget savvy and ask if there are differences in price depending on the day of the week or time of the year—prices do vary. Ask them how many staff members will be working on your event. If the venue comes with an in-house caterer, you want to make sure there are plenty of servers to provide excellent service. Two servers per ten guests is an acceptable ratio, with another person busing and constantly keeping the table presentable. If trays of hors d'oeuvres will be passed by waitstaff among your guests, you want the number of servers to be equal to one-third of the number of guests (so for fifty guests, you'd want about sixteen servers), and at least two bartenders per fifty guests.

If you fall in love with a venue because of its view, always ask the folks in charge if that killer vista is expected to change—will there be construction or changes to the sight line that they might be privy to (but wouldn't volunteer unless asked)? It is a shame to choose a spot that has a magical panoramic skyline and have it changed at your party because of construction schedules. If the venue contains an outdoor social area, make sure there is a contingency plan ready to be put into place in case of bad **weather.** For example, does the venue supply **tents,** flooring, **awnings,** and **outdoor heaters**? If the venue doesn't offer these items, ask the staff who they recommend so you can deal with a bad weather situation yourself.

The Blank Canvas Space

As an event designer by breed, I love venues I can manipulate any which way, light up in any color because the walls are white, or lay down whatever flooring because there is no existing carpeting. This is a real luxury for me—and for my clients by extension! I did a party for Target once whose budget was not so great. To get the biggest bang for the buck, I just lit the walls, floor to ceiling, a glowing red—the store's signature color. The blank space was completely transformed, and it was so easy to do with colored lightbulbs and floor **par cans** that had red **gels** on them.

Large Industrial Spaces

These tend to be load-in friendly—some of these places even have elevators your truck can drive right into for delivery. This makes an event producer happier than anything and can save on labor costs. We produced the product launch for the Nissan Z years back, and not only did we need to display the new car, we needed to get it into the space! So we found an urban, rugged warehouse that really fit the industrial concept of the party and worked on a practical level too.

Top Floors

I love being high up in the sky and watching the city or nature through big windows. It's amazing to see the sun going down (or in some cases, coming up) as the evening progresses. This is nothing more glamorous than a space like the Rainbow Room at the top of Rockefeller Center or one of my favorite downtown lofts, the TriBeCa Rooftop, because both have the spectacular backdrop of New York City. On the other hand, the Bacara Hotel in Santa Barbara has an ocean view that can make you cry! At a New Year's Eve party, I wanted to be sure the guests could see the beautiful starry sky and cityscape. So we waited until midnight to do a dramatic opening of the window treatments and pow—the city was sparkling, almost as if it were planned just for the guests. A lot of people got midnight kisses, I think.

Castles

I designed an event for Bud Lite beer at Oheka Castle on Long Island. We wanted to celebrate the old-school brand of Budweiser in an old environment but with a new twist—so we lit the space with light blue and had a young, urban guest list. We used mod Lucite dowels instead of flowers in big silver trumpet vases. Castles are a great opportunity to be eclectic and mix modern touches with a conservative background.

Caves

Believe it or not, I once did an alarmingly beautiful wedding in a cave in Jamaica where we used candlelight and low tables with floor seating. The environment was so secretive and simple, it took my breath away—even when a bat took a dump on me, it was still magical.

OFF-THE-BEATEN-PATH PARTY SPOTS

Do you have a friend or family member with a nice big tract of land? Visualize a secret clearing in the woods where you can create a natural oasis with lanterns hanging from trees and an intimate family-style dinner. This kind of outdoor environment makes me think of fireflies—mimic their beauty by hanging bottles containing little LED lights from trees with fishing wire. Since the kitchen is probably far away, you will need to set up a cook camp nearby. Think upscale barbecue, with a couple of hibachi-type grills (instead of a big gas number the size of an RV) roasting up some sweet ears of corn, spareribs, and Cornish game hens. This type of environment

Tiny LEDs in hanging votives create a beautiful firefly effect.
ANDRE MAIER PHOTOGRAPHY

is obviously intimate—you can't escape each other when you are stranding yourself voluntarily in the woods—so reserve this space for celebrating your nearest and dearest. You could do a roast or toast for someone special—maybe a recent graduate, a birthday girl, or someone who is dedicated to a charity or a cause. To make this easy, use items you can throw away or recycle, like paper or plastic goods. For seating, use individual cushions or camping chairs that double as backpacks that your guests can carry to the clearing.

I must have been a horse in a previous life because I love the beamed ceilings, loft, stables, and impressive front doors of a good old-fashioned barn. Send the animals out for a spa day and trick out your barn by adding soft textures to the rough environment. Throw down a shag rug in the hay and use a long rustic farmhouse table coupled with some bench seating or an eclectic mix of chairs taken from your house. Your centerpiece can consist of cool eggcups, birds' nests constructed out of twigs and twine, candles, and other natural beauties. Or for a gorgeous twist on the trough idea, fill a long planter with water, and float flowers and candles in it for a delicate table display. If the barn has a loft, staple some heavyweight fishing wire and let it hang down from the ledge and attach more birds' nests to it or mason jars with votives inside. Make sure any open flame is at least a foot away from any flammable surface (basically everywhere in a barn), and that any candles are well below five inches from the top of the container. Put a tiny bit of water in the bottom of any holder containing a lit candle—this helps with wax cleanup and fire control. You can also use tealights that melt in their little metal cup

This wedding held its reception in a 140-year-old barn in upstate New York.
ANDRE MAIER PHOTOGRAPHY

always conjure up a vision of chicks in high heels with major girly drink buzzes ending up splay-legged at the bottom of the stairwell. Steps are simply not nice to old people, and by that I mean anyone over the age of eighteen. They are also a nightmare for the waitstaff trying to serve trays of pigs in a blanket or überspillable cocktails. I get heart palpitations just thinking about it. Legally, a venue is obligated to offer

containers. Tealights last from four to six hours at the most; a regular votive candle can last up to ten to fifteen hours. If fire is not your thing, battery-powered LED lights are a very safe bet, though more expensive. LED lights are about $2 a piece versus a votive candle that can run as low as 35 cents each. If you have any friends who play the violin or guitar, it would be amazing to have that as background dinner music. If your crowd is a bit more hyper, then push the table aside and throw a hoedown that would make the farmer in the dell smile.

THE WORST LOCATIONS: BEWARE OF THESE PARTY TRAPS!

When scouting out a location, I shy away from several things.

Steps and stairways repel me—especially spiral ones. They

These delicate votives are hanging from the branches of a centerpiece.
ANDRE MAIER PHOTOGRAPHY

Stairs can double as an obstacle course at your event. ANDRE MAIER PHOTOGRAPHY

elevator or ramp access options, but these are usually reserved for folks who truly need them, like people in wheelchairs. Plus, elevators can only hold a few people at a time, which can create weird bottlenecking in awkward areas of your party.

If you throw an event in a space with low ceilings, you may as well throw a party at Alcatraz and call it a day. Putting a load of drunk, dancing people into a low-ceilinged room is like me trying to squeeze my ass into a size 2 pair of jeans—no one should witness that. You want to give people room. A party should resemble a freedom-filled vacation where folks come and forget all of the bullshit in their lives for a few hours and become the happy kids they once were.

If your venue or home is stuffy and doesn't have a lot of airflow, then the only food you should serve is oxygen. You don't want folks becoming exhausted from just standing around. Air equals energy and allows your guests to last the night and not want to leave after the first ten minutes.

Fact of nature: We all gotta go, so having multiple, accessible, and working bathrooms instead of not enough potties at your event is a beautiful thing. If one bathroom retires early for some reason, it's great to have a backup, such as an external toilet you can rent, or allowing guests into your inner chambers and letting them use the VIP master bath. However, I tend to steer clear of letting my friends tour my coveted sanctum and chance upon any embarrassing items I may have lying around. So it's probably best to rent a **Porta-Potty** from a local vendor.

Although a sunset dinner around a crystal lake where frogs and butterflies perform a synchronized swimming routine sounds like the ultimate setting, any kind of water will attract a shitload of bugs. You will be introduced to a world of creatures you have never seen before: bugs that look like big sticks, bugs that speak five languages, and bugs that just laugh as you apply your fifth layer of OFF! I hate biting into my burger or hot dog with the aroma of bug spray permeating every

Not enough potties = very unhappy female guests. DAVID PFENDLER

pore of my being—it just taints the whole experience—so if you want to be near water, keep yourself at least five hundred feet away from the shoreline to give yourself half a chance of enjoying the party.

• ● •

All in all, you need to go with your gut when choosing a venue—just as you would when buying or renting a home. Do you feel most comfortable entertaining in your own home, or does that feel like an invasion of your privacy? When you walk into a venue, pay attention to your emotional reactions to the space. These are important little voices to listen to that can sometimes be drowned out by the 50 mph sales pitch being thrown at you by the manager. Don't get turned off by small items that can easily be changed or ignored. Many places have existing carpeting that most people hate, but in the evening hours with all the tables and chairs in place, your guests aren't going to notice those shitty swirls. Your party location should be workable, budget-friendly, and (most important) make you feel excited and proud.

CHAPTER FIVE

Invitations
(Or, "I Never Knew Paper Could Be So Expensive!")

It makes me laugh when I think about how often people forget they have to officially invite guests to their events. They get all the tough stuff done—choosing a venue, picking a menu, all the details like flowers and guest lists—and then they skip the part where they actually tell people about the party. But obviously, getting the word out to people is a crucial part of this process, and increasingly it's becoming more significant *how* you get the word out. Your invitation can preview the concept for your event through its style, typography, and color palette. If I open up a neutral card with fancy black script on it, I know I may be attending a black-tie event.

If the invitation has a more colorful, contemporary font, I know the party will be looser in feel. It's a great way to tell your guests a little secret about where they are going and what they should expect to dredge out of their closets to wear. But it shouldn't just express the style of your event—it should express the style of *you*. To me, a truly successful invitation is one that illustrates to the guests exactly who is sending it, and they say, "This card is so Jes." There are many different ways of

A fancy scroll clues you in to the formality of the party.
ANDREW BICKNELL PHOTOGRAPHY

inviting folks to a party and aside from shouting relevant info from the treetops or enlisting carrier pigeons, this process can be as simple (or as stressful) as you want it to be.

WHO'S COMING?

First things first: the guest list. I'm not a big believer in getting the right mix of people. We underestimate our friends and families when it comes to understanding who they will mix well with and who they won't. I adore throwing people together in a celebratory environment and watching them get to know each other regardless of their race, age, or religion—to me, this is what makes a party tick. Many planners would say that if you are having a heavy-metal party with a crowd of rockers, you may not want to invite elderly people or children, but I disagree with that way of thinking. Parties are fantasy and a chance to get away from your daily routine. You just might find a ninety-year-old man having a wonderful discussion with

a twenty-four-year-old indie kid. We need more diverse environments in this world, not fewer! However, I do caution you to make the environment comfortable enough to accommodate the diversity of your crowd—that is, don't have the party in a skateboarding half-pipe if you're inviting the ninety-year-old man. The music or entertainment needs to cross the boundaries of your guest list and appeal to everyone—so mix a little Cole Porter in with that Guns N' Roses. Case in point: I recently attended my father's seventy-fifth birthday brunch with a very mixed guest list: ten adults and fifteen children under the age of ten. My first instinct was to pop several Xanax and ride through the mania, but it turned out to be a blissful day because we made the environment suit both age groups. We had an adult table with a lovely floral centerpiece and well-deserved mimosas. The kid's table was filled with an assortment of crayons, markers, paper, stickers, and tape—

and these kids went to town! We also borrowed a small television to play a loop of *Happy Feet,* and we ordered the kid's food first so they wouldn't get antsy while the adults talked. We had a variety of tunes, from Johnny Mathis and Nat King Cole to *Veggie Tales* and *High School Musical.* The day went swimmingly, even though it was a very mixed crowd! You don't always want to push the guest list mixology *too* hard, though. If you know of existing drama between certain people, you don't want to use your event as a psychotherapy session that could ultimately make life hell for everyone.

Speak to feuding guests beforehand about the possibility of inviting their nemeses and see how they react—but honestly, it's up to them to work it out and you have every right to move full steam ahead. Remember that you are being gracious by inviting people to have a nice time, so you don't need to feel guilty or responsible for anybody. If your friends and family members

Don't tolerate feuding guests at your party—there's no room for catty fights!
DAVID PFENDLER

can't put away their issues for a few hours to respect you, you should perhaps rethink the quality of your relationship!

If you are paying for the event yourself and the budget is killing you (which is probably likely), you may be forced into shaving down your guest list. Create an A-list and a B-list; the A-listers are people you know you want to come, and the B-listers are those on the fence, like coworkers or old friends you haven't seen in a while. You can even stagger your invitations and invite the A-list first and only invite someone from the B-list when someone on the A-list can't make it. Remember, you aren't given a party quota in your lifetime. If you can't fit all your people into this party, you can have more later. You want to look around at your event and be thrilled about everyone who is there. You will get a lot of pressure from your mom saying you need to invite an uncle you haven't seen in a billion years—but if you are footing the bill, you have the final say on who gets an invitation. Even if you are not footing the bill but you will be hosting the party (and this gets very tricky), I firmly believe you should still have majority control over the guest list, relinquishing a percentage to the party funders. Picture a young woman getting hitched, and her parents want to throw her the wedding of a lifetime—but she can only invite ten of her friends while the rest of the guest list is Dad's business associates and Mom's tennis club partners—not cool. In this case, you should have a sit-down with your bankrollers before accepting the gift to find out what they are expecting in terms of the guest list.

In terms of numbers, factor in a 20 percent to 50 percent decline rate; if you are inviting one hundred people, it's relatively safe to assume that eighty to eighty-five people may actually show. But like a good Scout, always be prepared to host the full one hundred no matter what, because you may decide to use some of your extra invitations to give to some people who didn't make the first cut. If you are throwing an event where a lot of your guests need to travel to get there, your attendance may go down even further (out of one hundred guests, seventy to seventy-five may show). When choosing your venue, then, make sure that the difference of twenty or so people won't make the place seem like a tiny cave or an oversized stadium.

Then there are the guests who bring guests. On your invitation, make it clear whom you are inviting, such as Mr. and Mrs. David Dickerson; on your RSVP card you should write something crystal clear, such as, "Who will be attending this event?" This upfront question should help you with the head count. Sometimes people want to bring along a friend who happens to be in town. In this case, I would hope your friend asks you if that's OK with you; I usually welcome the diversity and say yes!

STDS—THE GOOD KIND

Depending on the scope of your party, you might have to start with a little thing called save the date. This serves as an advance warning to your guests to clear the date on their calendars so they can make travel plans, schedule childcare, or get the day off from work. These courtesy notes also enable you to get a sense of who is serious about attending your party, since you frequently get a response even before you bother with the actual invitation. The industry term for these notes are STDs (kind of gross, yes, but we need our little jokes). I dare you to go to a stationery store and ask for help with your STDs—if they return to the table with rubber gloves, you may be dealing with an amateur.

Save the dates are invitation Mini-Mes; they don't have to be as tricked out and should be less expensive than your real invitation. STDs come in many different styles from e-mails to **magnets** to **postcards** to a prop of some kind. Say you're

Jessica's STD was a vintage postcard of her wedding's home state location.
JES GORDON

having a clam and lobster bake—you could send out those paper bibs you get in seafood restaurants and print the info on them. I feel that because actual invitations are taken more seriously, it's fun to add a little humor or personality to the STD—but it should jibe with the tone of your party so that people don't think they are headed for a luau when it's really a black-tie affair.

One of my favorite STDs in the history of my career was from a young couple getting married during the holidays in New York City. They went all out on the save the date (in this case it was more expensive than the invitation but it was important to them). Their STD was a small white box. Nestled inside was a silver paper ornament with the couple's picture on it and the words "Take a Snow Day" and the date and location of the wedding. Alongside the ornament was a tiny Barbie-doll-size white vest. Later, many of the guests told me they used the vests as ornaments on their Christmas trees.

I want to interject something really important here: The post office is the boss, no matter what, so before you send anything through the mail, be sure to bring a mock-up to your local post office to see if it's acceptable and the price of postage is reasonable (guessing with Internet calculators doesn't cut the mustard). Different size envelopes take different amounts of postage; for example, square envelopes cost more to mail than rectangular ones, and since the postage rate for **stamps** seems to change every time we turn around, it's best to constantly stay in the know. If you are not diligent, you could be very disappointed to find many of your STDs or invitations returned to you—and then you have to spend a fortune sending them by FedEx or UPS.

THE INVITATIONS: FROM COMPUTERS TO CRANE

Once again, there is more than one way to skin a cat here. Let's

Jes's Invites to Remember

- We designed a great invitation for the launch of a new razor. Instead of paper invitations, we sent out gorgeous girls with long legs in short shorts who rode around Manhattan on pink Vespa scooters, personally delivering an invitation to each guest in the form of a razor with the details imprinted on it. This idea made quite an impression—the attendance rate was phenomenal, thanks to those leggy girls.

- For a one-year-old's birthday party invitation, we created a simple iMovie on a Mac made from baby pictures and a soundtrack of "When I'm 64" by the Beatles. After the thirty-second slideshow came a page with the party specs. This type of thing can be done with PowerPoint too—just e-mail it, send out a flash drive, or burn it onto a DVD.

- For a vodka launch, we sent out carved potatoes. Most people go the super-sexy model route with alcohol, but we had an artist carve the details into an actual potato, as one would using a lino block. You could even make potato prints this way if you ink them up. We sent the potato out in a box with scruffy tissue strands, much like a pet rock.

- There is nothing lovelier than using a child's piece of art as an invitation. To me, this is the most personal, charming invitation one can receive, because after the wow factor dies down after receiving a potato in the mail, all you are left with is the gimmick itself and not a treasured piece of original art.

- If you want your guests to remember your event, you could send out conceptual thank-you cards. We once did an urban awareness event for young twenty-somethings with a sex ed expert on deck talking about safe sex. To thank them for coming, we sent a replica of a condom package with a real condom inside—hopefully one they added to their already existing collection.

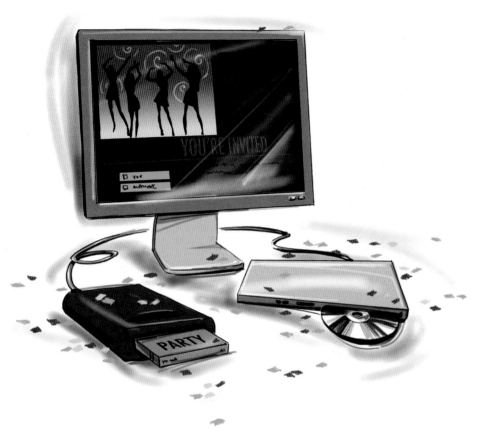

Evite—the fastest way to get the word out. DAVID PFENDLER

start with the easiest mode—the online invitation. Thank the Lord for online invitations! These are so cool and so unbelievably convenient, it's almost scary how lazy technology can make us—but I like to think it lets you relax and conserve your energy for the party.

The biggest behemoth in the biz is evite.com (although other cool sites I've found are pingg.com and socializr.com). At Evite, you can choose from the designs they provide, or upload your own fonts and photos to personalize it. Evite not only lets you invite everyone

by e-mail, it keeps track of your RSVPs, which is a whole other ball of wax. Usually one has to keep an Excel spreadsheet or some sort of ledger to keep track of guest counts and responses. Evite does this and e-mails you when any guest responds. I use Evite for a casual event, like a cocktail party, an office gathering, or a bowling or activity party. More formal parties need a more formal acknowledgment.

Another method for the technologically savvy is loading your information on a portable USB flash drive or a DVD. You can create a computer file of any type—a simple Microsoft Word document, an animation, a PowerPoint presentation, a Photoshop image, or a little movie with music and all the bells and whistles—and save it on a USB memory stick or DVD, which you can send out to your guests to load on their computers. The cool thing about a USB drive is that it's also a little geeky gift for your guests—after the party, they can always use it for extra storage space. (In that case, I would suggest getting drives with no more than 1 gig of storage). USB drives come in customizable colors and styles—you can get them with a logo or in the form of a pen, Swiss Army knife, a rubber duckie, or even a piece of sushi. Prices vary, depending on the storage space of the drive, but it's usually under $10 per gadget. If you go the DVD burning route, you can design your own labels very easily with labels and templates from avery.com. Now, your guests will have to know how to plug in a USB drive or play a DVD on their computer, so don't use this idea for a group of people who will be mind-boggled and frustrated by this—for example, your ninety-year-old grandpa who may have never used a computer. I think this kind of STD or invitation works best for a corporate party, or if you are a bunch of dorks having a Dungeons & Dragons showdown.

If you feel like all this computer garbage is just not your style, then feel free to kick it old school with some simple homemade cards. No, I'm not suggesting you whip out the dried macaroni and Elmer's Glue—making your own cards has become fairly upscale these days, especially with the help of the Internet. Web sites abound that help you upload your own photos and text into designed templates, which they print for you on nice-quality card stock; to find retailers, just search "custom photo invitations." (I think some good ones out there are vistaprint .com, americangreetings.com, tinyprints.com, polkadotdesign.com, and photo-sharing sites like shutterfly .com.) If you want to design your own invitation but need a little bit of guidance, good stationery stores like Papyrus and Kate's Paperie have invitation staff who will help you choose from their stock of nice paper and designs. Another cool idea is to hit up local art students for help; put an ad on a job-posting board at

a graphic design school in your area. Students are hungry to expand their portfolios, and they'll do it for beer money! (That's how I got someone to design my Web site.)

Another semihomemade option is to buy imprintables or fill-in-the-blanks boxed invitations from a stationery store or office supply store. Imprintables are precut invitations that you feed through your home printer; fill-ins are handwritten. If you're left-handed, I would skip the fill-ins, but if not, a cool colored-ink pen can cover up a few handwriting sins. However, if your skills are at the Neanderthal level, a fancy metallic Sharpie won't help you. Calligraphy pens are only useful for people who actually know how to write in calligraphy. I say, enlist Grandma. Eight out of ten grandmas (or great-aunts or other older female relatives) actually have wonderful handwriting—they learned to write in fancy script in school, whereas we've been ruined by computers. However, the

Cute Invitation Ideas

- **Beach party:** Create an invitation in neutral sand tones with touches of gorgeous blue that recall the colors of the ocean. Incorporate a lovely letterpressed motif of a seashell, sand dollar, or my particular fave, a sea horse! Some folks think it's cute to put some actual sand or other small particles like glitter or fairy dust in the invitation, but frankly, crap-filled envelopes are just one more reason to get out the vacuum cleaner.

- **Disco party:** The first thing that comes to mind is mirrors, perhaps expressed by a reflective paper border on the card or envelope liner. Or get technical and make a CD of favorite tunes with the party info printed on the CD label, which you can make at home with Avery labels.

- **Doggie party:** I wish the world had more of these. The most obvious emblem here could be a paw print motif. Once we did a really cute invitation for a pup's first birthday by creating a moving design out of construction paper in the shape of a dog's head—when you pulled its tongue, its ears popped up. (I have to admit that I enlisted a seven-year-old to help me out on this one. She had been making movable construction paper designs all summer at camp, and she rocked these out so fast, I still don't officially know how to produce them myself—so grab your favorite seven-year-old and hire the kid!)

- **Holiday party:** I can't even fold my laundry, but if a holiday party invitation came to me in origami form, I would pee in my pants. Something seasonal and wintry like a snowflake, star, or bird that your guests could also use as ornaments— how cool is that?

computer is a great thing if you're tech savvy—imprintables can look as good as custom made, as long as you load your paper correctly. Just practice lining it all up on regular paper so you don't waste the good stuff. Better yet, if you have a teenager lying around, get him or her to do it—say you'll make cookies later.

I suggest buying twenty-five more invitations than you think you will need, just in case some get lost in the mail, if you make new friends along the way and want to invite them later, or so you can invite the "second tier" guests that you couldn't afford in the first round. Here's the information you may need to include, depending on the intricacy of your event:

1. Date, location, and time. A tip about timing: Make the start time a little early, like 6:30 p.m. for a 7:00 p.m. party. By the time people show up, say their hellos, and settle down, it'll be seven o'clock and you're still on schedule. If people are late, keep the party moving. Unless your guests got hit by a truck, it's rude to be late and they need to suffer the consequences, not you. If they miss dinner, they can still join in the conversation and drinks and hit a burger joint on the way home.

2. The type of event, for example, wedding ceremony and reception, cocktail party, product launch, or birthday party.

3. The names of the host(s) and the guest(s) of honor.

4. Specify guest quantities (i.e., plus ones).

5. The attire, if you are specifying.

6. A reply card with a self-addressed, prepaid envelope, or just a reply card, self-addressed and prepaid. On the reply card, ask guests to specify how many in their party will be attending, so you can keep a head count. If you're serving a meal and not providing a separate menu card, put food choices on the reply card as well, or provide a place where guests can specify any dietary restrictions. The reply card should also have the deadline date for regrets—ideally, a month prior to your event.

7. Directions from major thoroughfares.

8. Local accommodations, from high end to budget conscious.

9. Available transportation, such as nearby airports, car rentals, subways, trains, buses, boats, or ferries.

10. Contact info (phone and e-mail) for a key person who can answer general questions. Most of the time, this is for the host or an event planner.

Let's say you're having a formal party with custom-designed invitations—high-quality paper stock, engraving, RSVP cards, the works. You want your invitation to express the feel of the event, so when choosing your design, don't just opt for the conservative Crane or Cartier style with engraved black script on an ivory card—particularly if your event is going to be at a roller disco. You want to express the style of your party—and your style as a host—through the paper, fonts, and colors. However, the process of designing the invitation can make some folks go criminally insane, so here are some tips to get you through the task.

The world of paper—its thickness, its color, its sheen, or even its shape—is seemingly boundless. Most invitations are printed on card stock, which is heavier than regular paper. Card stock thickness is often described by pound weight, usually in the range of fifty pounds to one hundred and ten pounds, and its thickness is usually measured in

points, from eight to twelve points. You want to choose a paper that is thick enough to survive the postal trip, but if it's too heavy, then your postage price goes up. You want your paper to be able to stand up to production standards, meaning they won't rip easily while they are being cut, or cause ink smudging because of a slick surface. I think going with a midweight paper is A-OK. A card stock in the sixty- to eighty-pound range will hold up, but still fold easily. One hundred to one hundred and ten pounds is considered heavier-weight card stock that is extra durable. Technically I am a bit of a paper whore and tend to use very nontraditional papers, like faux alligator skin, faux wood grain, faux suede, faux patent leather, vellum, and metallics, but they are not always practical choices. These papers are not printer friendly, but they do jibe with more expensive and custom options like embossing or letterpress by a professional. If you want to get glam with paper

but your budget won't allow for it, a good compromise is to print the invitation on normal card stock and use the funky paper as a border or envelope liner only. Card stock does come in different textures too, so it's not like you're being a dud—you can get linen, pearlescent, sparkly, or recycled versions with a lot of texture. The color of the paper is pretty much up to you, but keep in mind that you want folks to be able to read the writing on the wall, so pick a hue that allows the script to stand out. I like soft beige- or ivory-toned papers because they're not harsh on the eyes and absorb color nicely. The average price of a piece of card stock can range anywhere from 35 cents to $2 per sheet (and the glam papers can start as high as $5 and up), so if you are producing many invitations, you will need to compute wisely. Four-color printing is also something to be aware of when pricing your invitations. This means that the invitation is produced in four

Nice Color Combos for Paper and Ink

With color, it's best to start simple and work from there. Sometimes it's as simple as using ivory paper instead of white or using chocolate brown or navy blue ink instead of black. These colors are still in the classic zone even with these small changes—like changing a black-and-white photo to sepia.

Color can get overly trendy. For a while, every wedding invitation we helped design was powder blue and chocolate brown or celadon green and chocolate brown; I started to dread these colors, even though they are technically gorgeous. Sometimes these novelty colors don't stand the test of time, like when you paint a wall in your house and months later you wonder what pills you were on that made you paint your kitchen kelly green. To avoid this color walk of shame, start with an organic, neutral base like ivory, beige, or pale gray and then pop out a more vibrant color on top.

Wording Etiquette

I am a little bit of a rebel when it comes to this stuff. I find it odd when I receive an invitation from a dear friend that reads: "The honour of your presence is requested at such and such a time"—what the hell? This isn't how my friend normally speaks to me. I wouldn't suggest, "What up, shizzle? Wanna party?" (unless that is the way you normally speak), but your words in the invitation should reflect your personality, not Charles Dickens's.

I designed my own wedding invitation with the wording: "Join us in celebration as Jes Gordon + Bill Marmor are joined in marriage." I chose not to write Miss Jes Gordon and Mr. Bill Marmor because it is simply not us, and our friends and families know that. I used the plus symbol rather than writing "and" because, once again, that's just our style. Even though this wedding was very important to us and we it was quite glamorous, we didn't want to create an overly formal atmosphere.

However, if you are throwing a charity event where you won't even know half your guests, you should use their titles until you get to know them better, such as Dr. or Ms. If you like the way it looks to write out the word "Doctor" rather than abbreviate it, do whatever you think looks best or connects with the style of your invitation. The decision may boil down to having too many letters on the envelope or that your calligrapher will charge you more—just go with your gut on this. Also, it is always OK to use Ms. if you don't know what to call a female guest over the age of eighteen. If you are inviting young women under the age of eighteen, it's safe to go with Miss. If you have married friends who didn't take their spouse's name, make sure to invite them separately, for example, "We invite Jessica Baumgardner and Irad Eyal to this special occasion."

ink colors rather than a simpler two-color process, which does mean extra cost for you. By using colored paper, you can eliminate the four-color process since an existing color is already provided with the paper. Always consider a two-color option rather than four if you are working with a restricted budget. If you are feeling green, I always recommend incorporating some recycled paper into the mix whenever you can; paper-source .com has cool recycled invitations to choose from. Some new companies specialize in using alternative paper sources and toxin-free ink as an eco-friendly option; Smockpaper .com was the first company to offer invitations on luxury bamboo paper, and Typoretum.co.uk makes its invitations with vegetable-based inks and cotton fiber paper, a by-product of clothing production.

These days the average size of an invitation is ever changing. It used to be that an invitation should not exceed the size of a postcard because it was easier to mail—but now people want to distinguish their invitation from the pack. Usually they are four-by-six or five-by seven, but not always. You can choose a round or long rectangular shape, but remember you need to estimate higher costs on these types of invitations that require special cutting, envelopes, and postage, like die-cut invitations in the shape of golf clubs or martini glasses.

There are fonts out there to suit every person—contemporary, script, even graffiti. Despite the world of choices, try to rein yourself in to those your guests can read easily. The smartest thing to do is to go on the Internet and view as many choices as possible and see if any of your choices match up with those that your invitation provider can offer. Most of the time invitation specialists can get their hands on whatever font you suggest. I gravitate toward modern fonts, even if they are in script, just because they are easier to read, but there are some swirlier choices out there that are not only legible but stylish.

Favorite Fonts

Andale Mono
for an afternoon beach party

Bodoni
for an Italian-style family dinner

Bradley Hand
for kids' parties

Copperplate
for any kind of party

Eurostile
for chic fashionista parties

Georgia Italic
for a ladies' lunch

Helvetica Neue Light
just for the hell of it

Lucida Handwriting
for a twenty-fifth anniversary party

Snell Roundhand
for a formal wedding or even a one-year-old girl's birthday party

There are several different types of printing styles to choose from,

These gorgeous escort cards were calligraphed by a handwriting specialist.
ANDREW BICKNELL PHOTOGRAPHY

as well. Printed invitations can be engraved, letterpressed, or flat. Engraving is when the wording is etched into a copper plate in reverse, and then pressed onto the paper, leaving the raised lettering to be inked. It's the most formal, most time-consuming, and most expensive style of invitations out there. Letterpress is printing text with movable type, leaving sharp impressions in the paper—it's less expensive than engraving, but still nicely old school. Next in line is offset flat printing, which offers high quality at affordable prices. Last, there is laser or ink-jet printing, such as what you have with your home printer.

After you've designed the package, you need to design the wrapping paper—the envelope. Formal envelopes are handwritten. If you like the handwritten touch but your scrawl looks like it did in third grade, hire someone to address your envelopes for you.

This is done by patient and talented people who have mastered the art of calligraphy—or just have weirdly excellent handwriting. They usually charge about $1 per line, so that's about $3 to $4 per envelope. If you hire a calligrapher or use a funky font on your computer, it is very important that the address is legible. You don't want your mail carrier to need a degree in code cracking to get your invitations safely into your guests hands. You can also feed envelopes through your printer, but be sure to do a few test runs with less-expensive envelopes so you don't waste the good ones. Another option is to print addresses on clear envelope labels. And always remember to include a return address on everything you send out. If these babes get lost in the woods, they need to come back to you. I mentioned blinging out the envelope with fabulous paper liners earlier—that's a great way to inject a bit of style. As far as licking goes, you may want to give your tongue a little R & R by buying a glue stick or a moistening sponge to seal these puppies. You can also get some cool stickers (check out moo.com, which will create a slick sticker book of ninety custom stickers for $9.99 plus shipping). You can also get all Bram Stokeresque and have your very own wax seal made to your liking through a stationery store or an online dealer.

Don't ever let me catch you purchasing your invitations without seeing a proof of the design first! Usually if you're working with a specialist at a stationery store or designing an invitation through a Web site, you can preview a proof of what your finished product will look like. If you OK a proof, yet you still don't like the finished product, you will most likely be liable to cover the cost of the original invitation—even if it ends up in the garbage—plus the cost of the new batch. So put your granny glasses on and check the

wording, spacing, and color choices on those proofs very carefully. And just as you would with a scary diagnosis, it would be ideal to get a second opinion when proofing your invitations. Pick someone with an attention span longer than your average flea to take a good hard look at your proof to make sure it doesn't have any mistakes.

When purchasing an invitation package, it is common for the provider to want a deposit of 30 percent to 50 percent before starting production, and then you pay the remainder when you receive the invitations. They usually take four to six weeks to produce, so keep that in mind when ordering them. You may be pleasantly surprised and receive them on the early side, but don't count on it.

SPEEDY DELIVERIES

Timing, of course, is a super important factor. You don't want people getting their invitations too early, or they'll forget all about it

when the big day finally arrives—but wait too long to send them out and people are already booked. Ideally, you want to time it so people can chill with it a little and respond in a timely manner—say, a month and a half to two months before your event. (Obviously if you are having a casual get-together and inviting folks last minute, many of these guidelines do not apply.) Get yourself acquainted with a calendar to see when holidays are happening this year, and plan strategically around them. We have the big Hallmark holidays, like Christmas, Hannukah, Easter, Passover, Thanksgiving, and so on, but there are many other holidays nestled in between that should be considered as well, such as the Jewish holidays that occur in the fall and widely observed holidays like Labor Day, Fourth of July, and Martin Luther King Jr. Day. If your party falls on a holiday weekend, it's best to give people more time—like six months. I know that sounds anal and crazy, but because of money crunches these days, people make travel plans so far ahead that the early bird really will get the worm. Once again, this is why an STD is genius, because it warns people that an event is coming their way but you don't have to go whole hog that early.

If you are throwing the party of a lifetime, it may be emotionally difficult when it comes time to let your little invitation birds out of the nest and hand them over to the vagaries of the U.S. Postal Service. It's a control thing. But chin up—for the most part, our postal system is pretty awesome. It's safe to say that if you're mailing your invitations within a city or town, your guests could possibly receive them the same day if they are picked up before 10 a.m. If not, your local guests will receive them the next day, or at most, within two days. Invitations sent to other cities will arrive in three to five days, and international air mail will arrive within a week. I'd pad this timeline by a couple of days if you're

mailing invitations around a busy holiday, like Christmas. But it's really been my experience that the holiday rush makes the postal system work even better than usual (post offices have extended hours, hire more workers, and offer more mailing supplies during this time, after all). If you want a definite guarantee or timed delivery, you may want to spring for priority mail, FedEx, UPS, or DHL deliveries. As I mentioned earlier, it's very smart to bring large mailings of importance into the post office to get weighed and measured to ensure that you have the correct amount of postage. But don't get your invitations stamped with a meter—too generic and industrial. Design your own stamp at stamps .com, or go with a cool design choice only available behind the post office counter.

If you find that people are not RSVPing by your requested date, it's fine to shoot them a friendly e-mail or note to confirm that they got the invitation and to inquire

about their availability. When composing your guest list, collect their e-mail addresses too—it's really useful to be able to quickly send out info to everyone regarding major changes in time or location. It's also perfectly acceptable to ask on the RSVP card for an e-mail address. A quick note about RSVP wording: I don't like saying "Regrets Only" because requesting half a response invariably causes people to laze out and not respond at all. When you ask for yes and no responses, you get a firmer idea of numbers because yes responses tend to come right away, whereas the nos tend to trickle in more at the last minute—people trying to switch around their schedules or those who are on the fence.

SIMPLE DESIGN TRICKS TO MAKE YOUR INVITATION STAND OUT

Try paper folds. Instead of the regular bifold, you can have trifold invitations, where both sides of a three-panel piece of paper are folded into the center, or accordion-fold invitations, which have two or more parallel folds that open out like a fan into a longer document.

Make a flip book. Make an animated flip book of your invitation at Web sites like flippies.com or flipclips.com, which converts images or film clips into quick flippable books that everyone loves. You can use illustrations or just words to give your guests an interactive treat even before they get to your party.

Add texture. If you're stuck with a plain invitation, add interest with a textured border of faux fur, patent leather, ultrasuede, acrylic, or feathers. Embossing invitations creates a nice textural interest, and you can have words, monograms, patterns, or simple motifs pressed into the paper. You can also do something as simple as gluing a small crystal or mirrored dot next to your guests' names or emphasizing key words like the host's name in a special raised ink. Go and check

Jes's letterpressed wedding invite has an embossed ghost pattern in the background. JES GORDON

out invitation sample books at a stationery store rather than viewing them on the Internet, so you can experience the textures before you make your decision.

Think layers. I love ghost patterns, which are faint patterns in the background of the invitation. This underlayer causes guests to take a closer look at your invitation instead of just dumping it onto the growing bill pile. This pattern could simply be small polka dots, a wood grain design, or even a family crest. It's also really attractive if you are celebrating a certain person's bar mitzvah, bat mitzvah, or birthday to write his or her name as a ghosted image behind the text of the invitation—or, even better, letterpress or emboss the name into the paper, which gives the invitation more texture.

Be clever with words but not too clever. I have seen really fun word plays on invitations like one long continuous blurred-together sentence with certain words bolded; when those are read together, you get the specs of the party. Or crossword puzzles that map out the party details. But there is a difference between letting your guests be interactive to get them excited about your event and having them just get plain old pissed off. If you have any doubts about whether your clever idea is too clever for your guests,

just put relevant info smack dab in the middle of the paper so your guests don't need to guess where they are going and when.

Personalize the envelope. Make sure that the outside of your invitation doesn't resemble junk mail—meaning, use a nice stamp and write the address by hand. If you want to use address labels, then make them distinctive by using ones with colors, borders, or designs so the envelope looks personal and not officey. If you choose to use a sticker or a custom wax seal to seal your envelope, that will also hint to the recipient that this is a special piece of mail.

• ● •

To wrap up, remember that invitations are only a small part of your party. Since there are such great design options out there, it's tempting and easy to get carried away and blow your budget on this preliminary step. Remember

that you will have many chances to express yourself artistically at your event, so you don't need to feel like your invitations are the be-all and end-all. If you are at a loss, know that less is always more in this field—you can never go wrong with simple black text on a cream card.

CHAPTER SIX

Design: Bringing Your Wacky Ideas to Life

Lighting, flowers, decor—these are all the little things you think about as a host, but your guests wouldn't notice unless there was something missing. Think about it: How many times have you been at an event or restaurant and the ambience is just . . . wrong? The lighting is hospital bright. There are no tables to rest your drink, or there is a plethora of uncomfortable chairs. There are too many people in one small room, or worse, not enough people and it feels empty and lame. The air feels stuffy and the bathroom reeks. Designing your party space is about creating a perfectly balanced atmosphere, where people can step out of their everyday life and into a dreamscape where they don't have to worry about death and taxes.

Design is my first love. I love creating different environments

from scratch. A raw space is like a plain canvas you can transform in six million different ways—kind of like my mother did with her chicken dinners. It was always the same old six-pound bird, but Mom made that thing exciting by chopping, spicing, cooking, and presenting it in different ways. Same goes for parties—I think transforming a space into a world that evokes an emotional response from your guests is possibly the most important part of the party process. Design, really, is your concept brought to life—your ideas built from the nuts and bolts of decor, layout, lighting, and accents.

But before we get into those nuts and bolts, let's discuss some of my overall rules for successful event design.

MY DESIGN DOGMA

1. To create ambience, you have to appeal to the five senses all at once. One sense shouldn't outweigh the rest, or the balance of the room will suffer. In a perfect party world, you will simultaneously hit the pleasure buttons of sight (through lighting or stylish decor), scent (through natural florals, intoxicating candles, or good things on the stove), sound (through great music), touch (through textures, surfaces, and drapery), and taste (through food and drink). Think of these pleasure buttons as party aphrodisiacs. (For more on this, see "Setting a Sexy Mood" on page 108.) Since they are such large topics, we address music

Before and after: We warmed up this cold warehouse space with lighting and texture.
JES GORDON (LEFT); ANDRE MAIER PHOTOGRAPHY

and food and drink in chapters 7 and 8, but the other elements are discussed here.

2. Be eclectic in your influences, and don't get matchy—it's too boring. You don't have to have a room that only says cold, white, and sleek. Fill a room full of candles in a mod interior, and it evolves into something else entirely.

3. Know your audience, and design a space that everyone can relate to. Case in point: I once met with a mother of the bride to design her daughter's nuptials. The young bride works full-time and her mom was footing the bill, so really, the mom was in charge. However, the mom is about thirty-five years older, raised on Johnny Mathis, doilies, and bouffant hairdos. Don't get me wrong, she was very stylish—but her original influences were very different

I covered these traditional Louis XVI chairs with a funky zebra print for an eclectic feel. WWW.HENSHALLPHOTOGRAPHY.COM

from those of her offspring, which veered more toward Juicy Couture, Blackberries, and vegan cuisine. So not only did we need to create a gorgeous wedding design, we needed to marry their different styles in a cohesive way. The best way to do this is to come up with common denominators—in this case, color and texture. Everyone was in agreement that the hues should be deep burgundy and gold. When we agreed on this baseline, we were able to add design elements to

A clublike lounge area cozies up to classic dinner tables.
ANDRE MAIER PHOTOGRAPHY

to make your guests feel as if they crossed over to another dimension. Design your fantasy, but also make it recognizable so that it is apparent that the expression comes from you.

5. Make sure you don't sacrifice your guests' comfort to the design gods. Even small things, such as providing chopsticks instead of silverware for an Asian-themed party, could leave many of your guests starving at the end of the evening, so compromise by offering silverware sets (with bamboo handles, in keeping with the theme) and a cool pair of chopsticks to match. Believe it or not, these tiny ideas can really add to the design of an event while keeping it comfy for your guests.

appeal to mother and daughter: old-school standing candelabras filled with very contemporary mini burgundy-almost-black calla lilies. The combination was gorgeous. We also mixed the generations by adding a lounge area to a very formal dining room. Amid a sea of gilded tablecloths and dripping flowers, we designed a modern lounge by the **dance floor** outfitted with sleek Barcelona chairs, ottomans, and glass coffee tables. We accessorized with gold and burgundy pillows, throws, and plush carpeting so the party remained cohesive.

4. It's important to always think of design in a way you've never thought of before. You want

6. Even if you are throwing an event in your home that starts during the day and goes well

Offer your guests silverware at an Asian feast so they don't go hungry.
ANDRE MAIER PHOTOGRAPHY

into the evening, you have to go with the flow. The light and temperature will change throughout the event, so how cool would it be that when the sun goes down solar-powered lights automatically fire up, and the decorative pillows and throws added to lounge areas make them cozier as the night wears on? Simply lighting some fire pits or plugging in string lights you set up earlier can keep you in design heaven, no matter how long your event lasts.

7. Don't let your guests get bored experiencing the same environment for several hours. An ideal situation would be a multispace venue so guests can explore different areas, but if you don't have one, you can design a space in cool ways so it feels like many rooms in one.

• ● •

When I'm asked to design a space for a party, I try first to see how the concept can be reflected in every part of the design. To illustrate this in this chapter, I use as an example a birthday party we were asked to create for a ten-year-old girl. I noticed during our first meeting that she treasured a teddy bear she'd had since she was born. Let's not get into the fact she was still obsessing about this bear at ten years of age, but rather what she loved about the bear itself—it was soft as hell, made from this very plush chenille material. Bingo! In my mind, her event should be designed with soft textures because she loved them and they made her feel safe—and no one needed to know that this all stemmed from her teddy bear. This party, which was for kids and adults,

As a temporary fix, this pink carpet covered up a fugly concrete floor.
JES GORDON

DECKING OUT
YOUR FLOORS

First, you should look at the broader aspects of the space—the floors, ceilings, and walls. For the child's party, we covered the floor in plush

was to be held in a large photo studio and this is how we decided to transform its blank canvas.

carpet to warm the space up a bit. Any kind of carpet will always soften the space and aid acoustics as well. Carpeting is a real back saver too. Hard surfaces can really break the spine of your guests over the age of twenty-five after standing around socializing and dancing all evening. Warning: Carpet ain't cheap, but there are a few things you can do to

mitigate costs. Have a carpet provider measure the space and give you an estimate for a temporary carpet. This means it doesn't have to be bound, just cut to size and taped down at the edges to get through the event.

Choose carpeting that won't catch in women's heels and can take foot traffic and wine spills—that is, carpet that is lower grade and cheaper. Shag carpet is gorgeous, but it's a major tripping hazard; instead, use shag as an accent under a coffee table but not for the entire floor. Ideally, you want to go as ghetto as you can with carpeting: good old synthetic cut pile carpet. I love the natural look of sisal or jute but the stuff just can't take on a large event and it's expensive as hell. Berber is tough, but its price point is simply higher than your cut pile. Loop pile carpet can be affordable, but again, the loops are stiletto snaggers. Light colors, like white or ivory, create a lovely ethereal look, but in my experience it's best to go with a dark hue, like black, navy, or chocolate brown, so the floor simply disappears. Black carpeting is also the cheapest option. Your average black synthetic cut pile carpet will run anywhere from $1 to $8 per yard, whereas white or other colors usually start at $3 per yard and go up from there. Higher-quality carpets can run up to $45 per foot. If this cost is breaking your back, dark-colored **AstroTurf** is another option (yes, even indoors)—just make sure you tape the seams together so people don't trip. AstroTurf can run anywhere from 80 cents per foot to $15 per foot depending on your suppliers.

Throw rugs are another way to add dimension and interest to your floors. We once did a party in a large loft that had this pukey gray carpet. The party was at night so no one was really going to notice it, but I thought it would be fun to break up the floor space into different seating groups. We found faux animal print rugs at rugsdirect.com, overstock.com, and a West Elm

At this product launch, we were going for an '80s vibe—and voila! Fabulous zebra throw rug! ANDREW BICKNELL PHOTOGRAPHY

furniture store, and grouped them with lounge furniture and threw in some matching animal print accent pillows to boot. If you're having a house party, smaller throw rugs are a great way to change the look and texture of your space without having to invest a ton of money. A brilliant new company that has changed the floor landscape is FLOR (flor .com), which makes cool carpet tiles

in a variety of styles and materials. You buy FLOR per tile so you can create any size or design you want by mixing and matching. The tiles come in great poly blends that withstand heavy foot traffic, like from whiskery House Pet.

Floor mats or low-tack vinyl appliqués are another alternative to rugs. At a wedding, a couple wanted to use a family crest as a

A family crest floor vinyl livens up the sidewalk at a wedding.
WWW.HENSHALLPHOTOGRAPHY.COM

square piece with artwork on it, we have paid up to $1,000 for each vinyl—but it does offer a look that's off the beaten path.

For the truly adventurous, I also love creating area rugs out of wheat grass or sod; this especially complements an industrial space with hardwood or concrete floors. Lay down some heavy plastic matting before putting down the grass, because this stuff is moist and has lots of bugs living in it! The average flat of grass is about two-by-three feet and costs anywhere from $10 to $18 per flat. Do the math and make yourself the most organic accent you can imagine!

Lighting tricks are another way to rock out your floors. Instead of floor graphics on vinyls or creative carpeting, you can project shapes and colors directly onto an open floor space. We did a party in a beautiful outdoor location with tons of plush **furniture rentals,** but we didn't have any rugs to use. Our lighting designer used a **gobo** with a

design motif. Instead of carpets under the coffee tables, we had cool floor vinyls printed with their crest. Floor vinyls are made by 3M (the tape people) and any print store can look into this option for you. This product can take thousands of people walking or driving on it for days on end, and you can clean it easily. Just make sure your floors are super clean and smooth before you lay down the vinyls. Their low-tack adhesive lets you peel them up easily with no damage to the floor underneath; however, once you peel them up, they can't be used again. So it's not the most price-worthy way to go—for a six-foot-by-six-foot beautiful branch pattern on it that he used to project onto the floors where the seating was arranged—it was gorgeous!

TAKE IT FROM THE TOP: THE CEILING

If you're having an evening event, oftentimes the ceiling will disappear if you don't draw attention to it with lights. However, if your event starts during daylight hours, ceilings can be major eyesores. If you are dealing with a low drop ceiling like those Styrofoam Debbie Downer things found in drab offices, I usually cover it by pinning up cool paper. One of my fave paper stores for this type of operation is Paper Presentation in New York, but you can find neat paper almost anywhere. This task is made easier if you buy large sheets of paper or even rolls of solid-colored paper (which you can buy at photo supply stores, since they are used as backdrops at photo shoots). The specialty paper can be quite expensive (anywhere from $1 to

We hid lighting equipment with fabric panels and dangling decorative spheres.
ANDRE MAIER PHOTOGRAPHY

$15 per two-by-three-foot sheet) so the rolls of paper or even wrapping paper may be a better option for those large ceilings—they will cost more like $1.50 per yard to $10.00 per yard, depending on your choice. For the teddy bear extravaganza, we were dealing with a dreamy high ceiling, so we decided to

stretch panels of gauzy fabric across the entire ceiling. All the fabric was gathered in the center of the ceiling, where it all came together in a collection of large and small Styrofoam spheres (five-inch- to eighteen-inch-diameter balls bought at a crafts store) covered in plush chenille. We pinned the fabric to

We gelled each step a different color on this stairway to party heaven.
ANDRE MAIER PHOTOGRAPHY

the spheres with basic U-shaped hat pins. If you like the idea of draping fabric, I suggest using scrim, which is basic gauze on a big roll that costs about $1.50 per yard and usually comes in white or ivory. If you want something colored, a nice alternative is a sheer organza or chiffon. Organza and chiffon usually cost about $3.50 to $9.00 per yard; some of these fabrics have sparkles that reflect light.

LET THERE BE LIGHTING

Which brings us to the next large element to think of when designing your space: lighting. Use natural light, synthetic light done well, or, of course, candlelight. You may be lucky enough to have lots of windows with southern exposure, but make sure to hang a sheer curtain to soften the strong light. Light must be distributed around the space equally, like rays of sunshine hitting as many points in the room as possible. If natural light is not an option for your event, create perimeter lighting using simple par cans that sit on the floor. If you use amber-colored bulbs, then you can create a faux candlelight look. If you choose to use candles instead, remember they are rather dangerous—so be sure to encase them in a glass holder, lantern, or cylinder. Also, buy the candles with a ten-hour life span and easily accessible wicks to ensure long-lasting light. Use small lighting accents around the room to hide nicks in the plaster; buy some simple par cans at the hardware store and screw in any color light bulb. You can also gel any recessed lighting and change the hue of the room that way. Go one step further by projecting patterns of light onto the ceiling with a metal gobo cut in a star or abstract leaf pattern set over a par can. I'm also a huge fan of projecting animations on a wall or ceiling—I am not referring to Scooby Doo here (although that could look pretty cool). This is more about hiring a talented artist who could animate any design, from a picture of you to something more conceptual. I was once in a trendy restaurant bored out of my skull; when the sun went down, I noticed something breathtaking on the wall behind me—a projection of floral vines that slowly grew up the wall and bloomed into magnificent flowers. I was mesmerized. I thought, "How dope would this be at an event?" So, instead of the typical rehearsal dinner photomontage of you and your intended in diapers, have someone create an animation of your love story!

Now, back to the teddy bears. Because we were designing this party for ten-year-old girls, we saturated the joint in lots of different shades of pink lighting. We replaced existing lighting with pink party bulbs, and gelled the recessed lights in different shades of pink, from light rose to deep fuschia. My fabulous design director created a cool graphic of tiny abstract teddy bears, and our lighting designer projected it onto the wall in a repetitive pattern to look like virtual wallpaper. This softened the hard concrete edges of the walls. We also used lighting on the **dance floor,** which was elevated and constructed out of thick Plexiglass boxes held together by metal brackets. (Don't try this at home. A professional should fabricate this for you, or some party rental places may have them in stock, but the average rental price for this type of thing is around $10K. Yes, this was a privileged ten-year-old.) Lighting mechanisms were wired inside—either fluorescent tube lighting gelled in different colors or with **LED lights,** which is a more expensive option but way cooler since you can change the colors by remote control.

DIVIDING (AND CONQUERING) YOUR SPACE

Another macro way to look at the room's design is by restructuring its configuration. You want to allow at least six feet per person so the room doesn't feel claustrophobic and uncomfortable. But if the space feels too roomy, like a big airplane hangar, try creating alcoves, or little hideaway nooks, that can act as a getaway from a loud band, the crush of the crowd, or just simply a great place to have a quiet conversation with someone. An alcove is like a refreshing time-out. (This is especially useful if you're inviting some elderly types—they definitely need an escape hatch from the loud music of a party.) However, creating separate nooks for your guests at a party is a tricky thing: You don't want to exclude the rest of the guests and make them feel that they can't sit with the cool kids. All alcoves should feel open and face the rest of the event in an acceptable **fake feng shui** fashion. Alcoves should be an

This lounge alcove was tucked under the stairs in a huge venue.
ANDRE MAIER PHOTOGRAPHY

oasis of comfort—I like having large floor cushions, plush carpets, low seating, and a truckload of intimate candlelight. Bring the ceiling down with mosquito netting, hanging votives, or bundles of preserved grapevines found at your local flower shop. I have created hookah lounges at hipster parties that were so popular there was a line at the entrance! These areas should be comfortable, but not so comfortable that your guests prefer to stay there the entire evening and not socialize. Don't serve food and beverages in there—force folks to gather their goodies out in public. Lighting can be lowered in the alcove, but not so low to create public displays of sexiness.

For our ten-year-old girl, we decided to make designated areas for the kids and the adults—but coexisting in the same room. How do you do this in one large room? The parents did want to be able to keep one eye on the kids, so we created an open-curtained room divider that was a semiprivate entryway into the kids' area that still provided enough of a sight line for the parents to feel comfortable. If you don't have a naturally existing nook in your space, you can create one by using three walls of fabric known as **pipe and drape.** While the adults had normal square-shaped dining tables in their area, the kids had lower folding tables propped on milk crates. They sat on **floor cushions** and they loved it and were able to act like kids in there.

Creating separate areas at a party is all about creating the illusion of escape for your guests. You want to make sure that your guests stick around your event and not really leave the room, or else it'll look abandoned. Lounges, bars, and alcoves within a larger space will ensure that your guests remain pleasantly happy hostages all night. I also like to create lounges near dining areas so when your guests are stuffed from eating or want to get away from their table, they can recline and digest, Roman style, near the action. If you have a cocktail area at your venue or home that is in a different area than the main reception or dinner area, be sure to close that puppy up when your guests move into the next phase of the event. People get lazy and comfortable and sometimes have a hard time getting off their tushies, so prod them like cattle and don't give them the option to stay put.

Further break up the room with "satellite stations," which are small moveable stations or bars. You can provide a **specialty drink** or food at this station, like a candy bar, or you can create more of an "action station" where chefs can prepare foods in front of the guests, like French crêpes or sushi. When you have spots of interest sprinkled around a room, the guests will stick around the party longer and

I created an intimate nook using pipe and drape at this cocktail party.
JES GORDON

not get tired out. But dividing a space doesn't have to be a physical thing—it can be simply visual, too. I love using **color blocks** to delineate areas of interest in a room.

Feeling ambitious—and flush with cash? Another option is to actually build tiered levels, like mezzanines, within a larger space. Obviously, this is a task left to professionals and not a good idea

for Nervous Nellie hostess types. How rock star is it, though, to walk into a high-ceilinged space and see cool alcoves and lounging areas built up above the main party space? However, there are precautions you should always take to ensure the safety of your guests, like installing railings on the stairways that lead into these magical little areas and lighting the stairs as well. Plus, these

A sushi action station—good food and good entertainment for the guests.
ANDRE MAIER PHOTOGRAPHY

I *love* picking out seating options for parties—it makes me giddy like a schoolgirl, like I get to redecorate my dream house every two minutes. I've used everything from floor cushions to beanbags to thrones to round pod chairs that dangle from the ceilings— and here are my lounge furniture tips garnered from years of experience. I like beanbags for kid parties—kids are like Gumby and can still fold their bodies in crazy ways—but us old fogies would be stuck in one all night if we dared to plop our butt down. As an adult alternative, I like the large ottoman. Or, possibly, low benches covered with comfortable cushions or fabric can be used for seating and even double as coffee tables. (A while back, we found gorgeous low tufted benches covered in black satin for a party; our prop master sewed flat crystals in the tufts for a bling element. These benches turned out so lovely that we decided to use them as coffee tables with silver trays for drinks.)

observation decks don't have to be twenty feet in the air. You can make a difference by creating elevations of even just six inches! Like a swanky sunken (or elevated) dance floor. Floor levels are what I call *advanced party design* but when it's done right, your guests will be talking about it long after the party ends.

Finally, when looking at the whole room, pay attention to the natural focal points in the space. Maybe there is a large picture window that you should draw attention to by lining its ledge with moody candlelight. Or a large industrial ceiling that should be softened with fabric or lighting. When you've dealt with the glaring issues in a space, then you can safely move on to the pickier stuff, like furniture, accents, and flowers.

Designing a Mod Cocktail Party

1. Think simple—everything in the room has to be about clean lines, so no flowing fabric treatments.

2. Throw down some fab shag carpets in seating areas with oversized, high-quality beanbag chairs. Also, low, round ultrasuede ottomans topped with graphic pillows would look fierce.

3. Keep the furniture simple and monochromatic but not necessarily just white—explore brown, pistachio green, and yellow tones for that retro look.

4. Create a bold graphic pattern on the wall with vinyl appliqués or a projection. Think about the fun patterns you see in vintage midcentury wallpapers.

5. Arrange some giant chrysanthemums in Jonathan Adler–style ceramic vases.

6. Cut up the space with cool room dividers, like a self-standing one from Eames (or, more cheaply, from West Elm), or hang up some curtains made with flat, mirrored beads.

It is important to remember that although seating should be comfortable, it shouldn't be so comfortable that guests just want to loaf all night. Provide seating groups sparingly—you should have enough places to sit for a little less than a third of the guest list. For instance, if you're having a party for one hundred people, you don't really want more than twenty-five guests lounging on furniture at any given time. If it's a cocktail party or dance party, go ahead and position some smaller tables around so your guests have a place to put their drinks. Some of these tables should have a few chairs just for folks to be able to sit down, but you never want your free-flowing party to be stuffed with couch potatoes. Create furniture groupings that are conducive to talking—ideally, a couch, a couple of club chairs, a loveseat, two side tables, a coffee table, and accessories like a rug, table lamps, and throw pillows—arranged in a square so everyone is facing each other. If you're having a party at your home, arrange your existing furniture in this way to promote the flow of conversation. Never place furniture groupings so people's backs are to the party or they are facing a wall—they should be able to see what's going on at the party no matter where they sit, so place your furniture perpendicular to the wall, not parallel to it. You can also make some very comfy "pillow lounges" out of **floor cushions** and fluffy rugs, but once again, it's not easy for adults to get in and out of those situations. Alternatively, I have seen some great low rattan seating at IKEA and West Elm—lower than your average chair but not as low as a pillow. Ultimately, you just want to make sure your seating arrangements are safe and sturdy. I love rocking chairs, but never use them because of the possibility of crushed toes. I

This simple table is both industrial chic and rustic. JES GORDON

generally choose seats that are very basic, timeless, and hardy—like your average club chair—and I accessorize it in a style that fits the party. I have mentioned this before, but I highly recommend temporarily slipcovering your existing furniture for a different effect at your house parties. You may have all-white shabby chic furniture at home, but for your party you can pick any color or pattern you want.

AT TABLE

If your shindig includes a meal, your choice of a dining table (and table accessories) will say a lot about the look and feel of your party. And there are many styles to choose from:

You can use antique farm tables that are long and rustic with bench seats, lit-up Lucite tables, or formal oval tables for that *Last Supper* meets *The Great Gatsby* look. You can outfit your dining room with an extra-long, extra-high communal table, à la Philippe Starck's Asia de Cuba restaurant in New York. You can choose square or round, glass, wood, or steel, myriad small tables or one big family-style table. You can even create tables on the floor with cushions as seating. I wouldn't suggest you cut the legs off your dining table, but sometimes you can unscrew table legs from the tabletop or fold them under. Then you can balance the tabletop on three sturdy milk crates—one on either side and one in the middle—for a sturdy surface. Add some linens,

a scattering of **floor cushions** or low ottomans on a comfy rug, and *boom*, it's an intimate dinner party, Japanese style. You can also rent light-up cubes made out of plastic or resin for your low table; even with a light linen, it would still glow ethereally. I don't know why, but I've noticed that when people sit lower to the ground, the evening takes on a more intimate, relaxed, and casual feel. If you choose to use a specialty table at your venue, be aware that most places don't keep that sort of thing in house—you're much better off using whatever tables they offer and spiffing them up with linens or other design tricks to make them come alive.

Dining chairs have become an industry all unto themselves. These days you can get custom slipcovers, chair back covers, chair caps that cover half the chair back, chair pads, and rental chair options that range from modern plastic versions, like the ghost chair or Bellini chair, to more formal ballroom chairs, like

the charivari chair. You can have folding chairs, bistro chairs, metal chairs, and wooden chairs. I allow that chairs should get their fair share of the design spotlight, but let's not forget the most important thing about a chair is its comfort. If you're renting chairs, make sure they will fit around the table to accommodate the number of guests slotted for that table. When making your seating chart, keep in mind the average tushy space for a chair is eighteen to twenty-four inches.

THE WORLD OF FABRIC

I mentioned before that draping fabric over a ceiling can really add dimension to your space, but the same thing goes for draping fabric on other surfaces, such as windows, walls, and tables. When you are in a perfectly square room, it is nice to create a fabric drape in the four corners with a sheer fabric to round out the room and soften hard edges. When working in a contemporary environment, fabric pulled taut and

Flame-shaped LEDs make this sheer stunning, but still safe.

perfectly smooth will create a more modern, clean, and contemporary look.

Accent a dark velvet curtain by attaching small crystals to the surface and lighting it with a spotlight—the drab drape turns into a gorgeous, glowing nighttime sky. I remember a bride saying to me that she wanted her wedding to look like the Delano Hotel in Miami—and since I've been there, I knew exactly what she was talking about. The Delano's lobby was decorated with floor-to-ceiling sheer drapes that blew lazily in the breeze and were anchored by candles in large glass lanterns. The place honestly resembled what I imagine heaven to look like! A flowing draped wall at an event is a beautiful thing, but the art of draping is not easy. Start out small in your own home by changing your drapery for the event to match your party concept. If you are having a cool cocktail party, then go with the Delano look and use those wispy sheer fabrics like organza, tulle, or scrim. To up the drama, shoot a light behind it.

You can buy standing floor **par cans** from Home Depot or a hardware store, pop in a colored bulb and aim them toward the wall,

Gray velvet curtains accented with crystal beads and ostrich feathers made for a dramatic entrance.

not the fabric. Be careful about getting the lights too close to fabric; use a low-wattage bulb, like sixty watts, and place it a full foot away from any textile. Quick safety check:

Stand over the light and hold your hand out. If it feels hot where you're standing, for God's sake, turn it off! Candles need to be in a glass container with the flame at least five inches below the container's opening. If you are having a more sedate sit-down dinner, try using a heavier fabric like velvet or an opaque shimmer satin fabric that will reflect light in the room. You can also build your own self-standing fabric wall from the aforementioned pipe and drape. Often pipe and drape is used to hide kitchen areas, dressing rooms, or just plain old disarray.

Fabric can also play a part in creating the ultimate wow factor at a party: the unveiling. I like to keep the special aspect of the party under wraps to keep some suspense going and create energy at an event. I've noticed that after guests have been at a multipronged event (meaning a ceremony or presentation, or a cocktail hour then a dinner), people get bored and exhausted. This is when the hosts need to light a new flame under their guests' asses. You can do this with pipe and drape by curtaining off the last party area and unveiling it just before for mega drama. Or you can do this simply with lighting: By lighting a cocktail hour in cool lavender tones and changing it to golden hues for dinner, it completely changes the environment. Something about having a curtained-off space drives people's curiosity wild—I've seen elderly ladies attempting to climb over banisters. Just make sure your veiled space is worth all the wait because those guests have to feel like they are entering Emerald City. I usually spend most of my decor budget on this last veiled space of a party, just so I can hear them catch their breath as they enter.

TABLE LINENS

Table linens are almost as varied as the tables underneath them. Simple flat cottons, linen, or hemp materials are A-OK for a daytime event, but for the evening I prefer linens with a shine or bling. This can be achieved many different ways: Some fabrics are naturally shiny, like a shimmery satin that is opaque but very glossy when the light hits it from different angles. You can use a sheer tissue organza or chiffon layered over a simple cotton underpiece. Many linens are already decorated and bedazzled with accents like crystals or sequins—or you can achieve this look at home by adding a border of sparkle to old linens that have lost their luster. Renting this type of shimmery overlay will usually run you about $40 to $100 per cloth.

One of my favorite party fabrics is silk dupioni, which has a lovely raw texture and multidimensional aspect because it's usually woven from two colors of threads. (Dupioni will look, say, orange in one light and hot pink in another.) Because it's silk, dupioni is opaque but still lightweight—and it frequently comes in a staggering array of vibrant colors. This is not

This moss-green dupioni reflected the light beautifully. ANDRE MAIER PHOTOGRAPHY

an inexpensive material, and it will run you about $8 to $30 per yard, but there is a great poor man's version—poly-blend silk shantung, which has the same slubbed look as dupioni but in a more economical and durable format. Getting this type of shantung will save you a good $5 per yard, maybe even more. Silk dupioni can be as fleeting as a one-night stand since it's hard to clean. If you're hoping to hang onto any party linens postevent, then you may want to check out the poly blends. Other

Rather than running lengthwise, these runners were placed in the other direction to shake things up. ANDRE MAIER PHOTOGRAPHY

fabrics that are rich and shiny are bengaline (which has a textural ribbed effect) and taffeta. Of the two, I tend to gravitate more toward bengaline; it's not as stiff as taffeta and hangs nicely on a table.

Make sure the linen fits your table correctly and hits the ground on all sides. If you are using an overlay, you need to make sure that the underlay hits the ground and that the overlay is about half that

length. If you have a slipcovered linen on a square table—known as a box-pleated edge—this should fit like a glove; otherwise it'll look as dumpy as a size 4 lady wearing a size 12 pantsuit. The box pleat is necessary because if the linen fits too tightly around the table, people won't be able to squeeze their legs under there. Pleats allow some give at all four corners.

If you're getting all Holly Hobbie and sewing the linens yourself, make sure you measure the diameter and height of your table. Example: If you are using a sixty-inch round table that can seat ten guests, your linen needs to measure one hundred twenty inches—just double the diameter of the table.

An easy, elegant way to bling out your table is to add a runner. If your budget only allows for a poly or cotton linen, a great way to add dimension (cheaply) is to lay a runner down the center made from fabric that has some sort of interesting texture. Depending on the table, the runner should only be about eighteen inches wide and run the length of the table and to the floor on both sides. You can go simple and have a cotton runner with a nice velvet ribbon border you can glue or sew on yourself. You can bring in a faux animal print like snakeskin or leopard or just use plain silk fabric in a wow color that complements the rest of your design. You can even use an organic material such as moss from your backyard, wheatgrass, pebbles, or even feathers! The runner is a great place to add a hint of eclecticism to the table. Just be sure that no matter what linen you choose, it is something that will feel nice against your guest's legs. Itchy or heavy fabrics mixed with bare female legs creates a hot, sticky, uncomfortable situation, so even though I adore faux fur and vinyl, it's best to keep them as runners only and not encase the entire table in them.

Also, be sure to put a table pad down before anything else. If

Simple but sophisticated is always a safe bet with napkins.
ANDRE MAIER PHOTOGRAPHY

you don't have a pad, you can use another layer of cloth to act as a buffer. Often rental tables have rough surfaces that can cause a nice linen to snag, and you want to muffle the annoying sound of plates, silverware, and glasses clanking on the table too.

AND NOW, ALL THE STUFF THAT GOES *ON* THE TABLE

With all the napkin choices out there, sometimes I feel like just

letting it all go to hell and handing out Brawny paper towels . . . but since we're here, let's explore some cool options. If you've gone the fancy route with your tablecloth, then your napkins should be more subdued. Go simple but high quality by using an old-fashioned hemstitched linen. If you want to keep the bling style going, you can have matching napkins custom made from your linen, but *always* back the napkin with cotton so people can actually use it to wipe their mouths! People generally don't want to wipe their faces with sequins. A good old cotton or poly-blend napkin is completely acceptable as well because, let's face it, the napkin ends up in people's laps or on the floor most of the time. It's also great to know that they are washable postparty. You can bring an old napkin to life by folding it in a cool way or adding a funky napkin ring into the mix—but again, keep practicality in mind. Don't fold the napkin into such a complicated origami sculpture that your guests need to be Rubik's Cube masters to actually use the thing. Also, don't knot any ties too tightly, like raffia or flower stems, or your guests won't be able to undo them. I personally have no patience for napkin folding, but there are great guides on the Internet if you're so inclined.

Charger plates, place mats, colored glassware, and fun place settings are a few other ways to bring

Faux-croc charger plates added glamour to this place setting.
WWW.HENSHALLPHOTOGRAPHY.COM

your tabletop up a notch. A charger plate is a larger-size decorative plate that goes under your normal dinner plate, which is usually removed once the first course is served. A charger plate or place mat comes in handy when you want the table to look gorgeous for your guests, even if there is no food on it yet. With your fierce centerpiece, candles glowing, and gorgeous charger or place mat,

the table doesn't look sad and empty. We have used charger plates that are clear glass but with gold or silver beads gracing the perimeter; or plain, colored glass plates in amber or amethyst tones; metallic plates in copper, gold, or silver; or even large rustic earthenware plates made out of slate or ceramic. Beyond the simple cotton variety, chic place mats come in leather, faux snakeskin,

"Tortoiseshell" tableware is rich and masculine—Ralph Lauren meets the jungle.

or croc skin, or as wooden or slate slabs that are smooth and treated with a protective coating.

These items can be found at many home furnishing stores such as Crate & Barrel, Target, Bed Bath & Beyond, and Williams-Sonoma. Colored glassware adds punch to the table as well, like placing an amber wineglass in the middle of more traditional hues. At one of our parties all the wineglasses were brown-flecked tortoiseshell to go with tortoiseshell votives we were using on the tabletop. Add some

Funky Napkin Rings

- For a kid's party, braid brightly colored yarn into loops.

- String marigolds together on clear fishing line for a spring tea.

- Glue acorns to the end of paper towel tubes for an autumn dinner party.

- Use vintage bangle bracelets for a bridal shower (bonus: The guests can keep them afterward!).

- Use colored rubber bands for a contemporary, clean look.

- Get eclectic by gluing different fabrics to paper towel tube sections. I like mixing and matching toile, Burberry plaids, and animal prints for a ladies' luncheon.

- Scour stores like Crate & Barrel, Pottery Barn, or Target to see what they have in plain silver, copper, or beads.

textured accents to your silverware as well, such as pieces with wood handles, mother of pearl, or even colored glass. All of these items can be used to tie in with the overall decor.

ACCENT-UATING THE ROOM

Like a coat of bright red lipstick, design accents can make what you have appear even more spectacular. Accents can be anything that adds oomph to a room, from throw pillows to curtain tiebacks. An animal print can add texture and interest, even something as small as a leopard pillow resting on a settee. I love to use accents with color, like tossing in a hot orange vase in the middle of a neutral-colored living room. It's also really striking to scatter oodles of colored-glass votive holders (like deep red or tangerine) in an all-white space and watch a stark room gain substance and intimacy.

Incorporating accents made from nontraditional materials adds warmth and personality to your event. A few of my favorite go-to materials uncommonly used outside the party industry are **aluminum foil,** which has a million decorative uses beyond food storage, and **alabaster,** an easy, elegant material that has myriad applications.

I love using mirrors to open up a space and create dimension within an intimate room. People love getting liquored up and hitting the **dance floor,** so provide a mirrored backdrop to let them check themselves out with their beer goggles on. Using mirrored objects, such as flower containers and hanging spheres, provides a natural light reflector; you'll get a bigger bang for your buck on any lighting, since it's bouncing off twice the surfaces. Just like in a hip bistro, install a collection of mirrors above a bar or your dining table so you can voyeurishly check out the guests during the party. Mirrored tabletops are cool too—have a mirrored piece of glass or acrylic cut to the size of your table and simply use the mirror in place of a linen. The mirror will

Double the pleasure: A bouquet of creamy blooms is reflected in this mirrored tabletop.
WWW.HENSHALLPHOTOGRAPHY.COM

accentuate your centerpiece, and even simple candles become stunning. Mirrored acrylic even comes in different colors, so you can go

An acrylic bar is backlit with a marine green. ANDRE MAIER PHOTOGRAPHY

crazy with a hot pink hue. Mirrored tabletops are not the most cost-effective option—count on spending at least $300 for your average six-foot table. Getting some reflective accents in the form of flower vases or candlesticks is a nice compromise, and this stuff seems to be in fashion at the moment. I have seen great mirrored accessories at Target, JC Penney, and Z Gallerie.

Cork or chalkboard is not only practical, it can also double as a funky design accent too. At one of our parties we created a long kids' table made with a runner of alternating squares of corkboard and chalkboard (easily purchased at office supply stores like Staples). The kids created their own decorative runner with art supplies we offered, pinning artwork to the cork and drawing on the boards with colored chalk. They suffered through the grown-up event, and afterward the kids could take home a favorite square or two to keep in their bedrooms. I've made napkin holders from chalkboard pieces—we wrote the guests' names on them and they doubled as fun place settings that people could take home with them.

I've also used corkboard to creatively organize seating charts for large dinner groups, like pinning old school pictures on a board for a twentieth high school reunion. (That way, people can see just how many dudes have gone bald.) Cork is a gorgeous material, actually, and I've seen it used as furniture, coasters, place mats, and candle holders. In this eco age, we'll probably be seeing more of it since it's organic and recyclable.

Finally, we come to one of my favorite design elements: acrylic. Everything that can be made out of glass can be made out of acrylic. Acrylic is lighter, costs about a third as much as glass, and comes in a gazillion colors. Acrylic is easy to cut, but it does scratch easily—that's why it's important to keep its protective covering on until the last minute. All those scratches mean that it can't be reused too many times, but it's still a much better value than glass. Why am I raving about this acrylic stuff? What does one use it for? *Everything!*

Acrylic comes in translucent or opaque gradients so it's fabulous for capturing light or acting as a solid backdrop.

Acrylic became very popular on the event scene not only because of its weight and cost, but also for its love of light—embed colored lights in acrylic planter boxes, bar tops, even **dance floors** to capture that celebratory *Saturday Night Fever* effect. With help from an event professional and a local industrial plastic dealer, you can build tables that can be lit from within, make huge chandeliers that are a cinch to transport, and create see-through chairs à la Philippe Starck's ghost chair. You can use scraps of acrylic to make hanging mobiles that will bounce light and create interesting patterns on the ceiling. As I mentioned previously, acrylic also comes in a reflective finish that is an economical way of providing cool mirrored surfaces at your party. Because acrylic is easy to manage by professional

plastic cutters, the corporate jet set has huge cutouts of their company logos hung and backlit on walls. For more homegrown events, acrylic can be used in the form of brightly colored, funky dinnerware (stores like Target and IKEA are great purveyors of this). Have sheets of acrylic cut into the exact size of your dining table or coffee tables and create colorful new tabletops that look awesome *and* protect your table. You can produce coasters to match and vases for the centerpiece too. To find local acrylic resources, look for companies with names such as Industrial Plastics or Plastic Mart—or ask a local contractor to hook you up.

GETTING FUNKY WITH FLORALS

Every party, no matter the size, needs an infusion of livid, blossoming beauty, or at least the organic touch of something living. This can mean anything from a casual arrangement on the table at a dinner party to more

I constructed a hanging display with acrylic platforms for invisibly suspending flowers in midair.
ANDRE MAIER PHOTOGRAPHY

elaborate creations. When asked to pick out flowers, hosts frequently get fearful and insecure, which always

An organic display made from pinecones, berries, artichokes, and wood-grain tableware. ANDRE MAIER PHOTOGRAPHY

surprises me because floral decor is one area where it's easy to do something outrageous, not break your budget, and make your event truly eye catching.

For a casual house party, I tell people to go into their yard and grab whatever catches their eye. It doesn't have to be a bloom, it can be some interesting long

grass, feathers, sculptural looking stones or branches, or any kind of greenery that's out there (except the poisonous varieties). Scatter them down the center of your table or artistically arrange them on some mirrored plates framed by candlelight and you've got a stunning centerpiece for free. I adore making table runners out of the bark from a birch tree or by using actual tree stumps of all different sizes as cocktail tables or even in thinner versions as place mats. I really dig rocks too! Flat rocks can be used for writing your guests' names in a metallic pen at their places at the table, or you can buy or find pieces of slate to use as place mats or coasters. Tree bark, moss, sand, and even dirt can grace any high-end event and add an unforgettable organic element. Just be sure to remove bugs and worms from these natural pieces of art!

When it comes to formal arrangements, I'm always a fan of using the more off-the-beaten-path blooms such as amaranthus. Not long ago, the idea of a near-black rose or a mini calla lily didn't seem plausible, but these puppies are now featured in the most coveted bouquets and centerpieces. Cotton branches are absolutely delightful. Let's not forget the gorgeous flower fritillaria, which comes in a provocative orange or maroon/brown shade. (Its distinctive feature is not only its beauty but its very strong olfactory resemblance to marijuana!) Some orchids smell like chocolate; others have stripes like a wildcat.

I love taking an average table arrangement and hanging it from the ceiling using invisible fishing wire or clear Lucite trays. Candles in hanging containers look like a magical floating dream. When it comes to floral decor, the sky is the limit—there's no reason to feel reined in by expectations. Even if you don't want to suspend them from the ceiling, flowers don't have to be arranged in a vase. One simple and gorgeous gardenia floating in a low glass bowl can bring me to tears. Or a simple dahlia head resting on each plate is a simple yet effective design strategy that brings your guests' attention to small focal points.

Hanging amaranthus gave this dining room a gothically romantic appeal. ANDRE MAIER PHOTOGRAPHY

Go ahead and get crazy by making your centerpieces multifaceted and varied in height.

Skip the rose bouquet. This varied centerpiece features moss and peacock feathers and tropical flowers (oh my!). JES GORDON

with another guest between stalks of bamboo. A great way to measure this is to put your elbow on the table and point your fingers straight up; your arrangement shouldn't be higher than your fingertips. You also want to make sure that your centerpiece doesn't drip into people's place settings—it sucks to have poisonous berries dangling in your butternut squash soup.

If you're determined to go high and mighty with your centerpiece, use taller pieces like candelabras or pillar stands that have a vase on top to hold the flowers. (I love constructing contemporary candelabras out of Lucite for this purpose. A plastic fabricator has to do this for you, but the outcome is very chic and impressive.) Make sure the base is clear and thin so guests can still see around it. With the taller arrangements, you don't want the tabletop itself to look bare, so create a cool candle-scape or smaller versions of the centerpiece around the main event. I like to use tall glass vases, say,

Take a collection of bud vases of all shapes and sizes, and cluster them in the center of the table with blooms—as a bonus, you can give a bud vase and bud to every lady at your dinner to take home as a parting gift. Remember when you are designing anything on your table, don't impede people's view of each other across the table. There's nothing more annoying than trying to discuss the upcoming elections eighteen to twenty-four inches high, turned upside down with a **Lomey dish** on top containing **floral foam.** Simply create a floral arrangement in the foam, place it in the Lomey dish on top of the overturned vase, and it looks like the flowers are floating in midair! You can even put stuff inside the vase, such as river rocks or rose petals, to add more interest down below. Stick some double-sided tape on the bottom of your Lomey dish so it adheres to the vase if someone happens to bump the table.

Another quick and easy contemporary floral centerpiece is to get clear glass vases of several heights and submerge an orchid stem in water in the vase. First, put some river rocks or beach glass at the bottom to secure the orchid stem, then nestle in the orchid, and fill the vase with water. Finish it off with a floating candle on top for a fast and not overly fussy floral display for a hip dinner party.

Small floral accents work well in restrooms, on napkins, tied onto chairs, resting on bars, coffee tables, end tables, and as small gifts for departing guests.

Use one large-headed flower, like a dahlia, peony, or gardenia, as a small accent—they have such gorgeous voluptuousness, you don't have to do much to make them look amazing. Sprinkle rose petals or cymbidium orchid heads along the center of your table around some candles for an easy organic touch. I once slipped three large hot pink cattleya orchid heads into each hanging crystal chandelier—there were thirty-six chandeliers in the room. The bright color amid the sea of crystals made the room pop so beautifully, and it was really simple. If you are placing stems somewhere outside a vase, be sure to provide water tubes for each stem so they don't wilt. You can buy water tubes from your local flower shop for about thirty-five cents each—it's worth saving a flower's life. We have taken flowers left over from large parties and

Ginger stems, submerged in water and tied down to river rocks.
JES GORDON

instead of throwing them out, tied them into takeaway bouquets for the guests. They love it! We do try to donate as many florals as we

Designing a Springtime Garden Party

1. Entertain in a room with natural sunlight, or even outside!

2. Create small seating areas out of patio furniture or old-fashioned wrought-iron tables and chairs.

3. Use potted plants, like mini potted roses, gardenias, and azaleas, for *everything,* including your table centerpieces. Hang potted ferns from above, and cover serving areas with natural moss accents.

4. Don't be afraid to get überfeminine and lush— use a lace overlay on top of your tablecloth.

5. For another centerpiece idea, grab a mismatched collection of vintage milk-glass vases and glassware to hold blooms. Go ahead and mix up your flatware, too, and serve your tea in an eclectic array of antique teacups and saucers.

6. Bring in some butterflies! They don't have to be the real thing, but place silk butterfly accents in all your plant decorations to create a realistic garden atmosphere.

can at the end of each event, but always check with the agency you are trying to bequeath them to; for example, hospitals frequently don't have the space to house them.

Plus, you don't always have to use flowers as your organic accent. You can make an awesome centerpiece from potted flowering plants like orchids; seasonal plants like begonias, gardenias, tulips, and mini roses; and for the holiday season, poinsettias and amaryllis. Poinsettias and amaryllis both come in new designer varieties, like peppermint, which is a red-and-white-striped plant, or even all white with splotches of pink that resemble a Pollock painting. Stay hip to the new stuff by touring a local flower market or forward-thinking floral boutique to keep up on the crazy hybrids that are coming out every year.

Don't forget to decorate the food display too—these little touches matter. We recently worked with a fabulously creative mother

Extra ethereal: white orchid heads swimming in clear water. ERIC HART

who was throwing her daughter a bat mitzvah. The concept was hippie-era peace and love—kind of *Hair* meets New York chic—and the mom made these cool colorful flowers out of felt that we stuck everywhere: walls, bars, tables, and more. We took her flower idea and made plastic hors d'oeuvres passing trays in the shape of flowers; the center of the flower was cut out to make room for dipping sauces.

The idea is to create food serving stations that are a natural extension of the rest of the room's design, but don't get so over the top that they impede access to the nibbles. I like using multilevels for food serving stations—even if they're just upside-down milk crates draped with fabric. Add a floral arrangement behind the food, or a fantastic vintage table lamp. I just found an antique gold Buddha lamp at a flea market that I plan on using on a dessert table for an upcoming event. Food presentation just adds another dimension of interest to your party and cause for conversation among your guests.

SETTING A SEXY MOOD

There are many forms of aphrodisiacs. For instance, when the Los Angeles Lakers win, I'm pretty sure that I'll be getting some in the near future. In the event world, the list of sexy elements is long—but not as obvious as people think. Some folks feel that if you have scantily clad servers or hired dancers who perform lap dances on the host, then the party will reach orgiastic Roman heights of coolness—but it doesn't. Most of the time the more obvious sexy touches cause confusion, insecurity and put a halt to any mojo that is brewing. You will be more successful if you simply work with the senses to create a sexy atmosphere.

- *Sight:* Keep the atmosphere dark enough so that people feel comfortable and secure, particularly on the **dance floor.** Make sure there are well-lit spots, though, so people can get their bearings. I often light restroom areas a little brighter so that the application of lipstick after the third martini actually lands on the lips.

These felt flowers worked their way onto food serving trays, too.
ANDRE MAIER PHOTOGRAPHY

- *Sound:* Paging Barry White! See page 121 in the "Music and Entertainment" chapter for a list of sultry songs to get sexy by.

- *Touch:* Only use the plushest and most inviting fabrics for your guests to sit on. Always use table linens or furniture coverings that would feel great on naked skin: velvet, cashmere, silk, sueded cotton—never anything stiff or itchy. Use thick carpets on hardwood floors, but keep it under control in high traffic areas so high heels can make it through. Throw a long shag under a coffee table for übersoft edges. Use large pillows or **floor cushions** so people can kick off their shoes and lounge—many guests welcome this after a few hours of surviving an event. Don't use overly warm fabrics; leather and vinyl might be sexy, but they don't breathe.

- *Smell:* Smell is nostalgic, and the sense of smell varies easily from person to person. I try to work with the seasons to create an enticing but subtle **scent.**

You can even add accents like table lamps to food display tables—there are no rules! WWW.HENSHALLPHOTOGRAPHY.COM

During the fall and winter, the smell of a fresh fire, cider, and roasting goodies in the kitchen can be all you need. Spring brings the bulb flowers, like hyacinth and paperwhites; they can be overpowering, but it if works for the birds and the bees, it can work for you. Summer is herbal and fresh—think mint and rosemary. Remember these scents exist naturally—simply push it a bit more by using scented candles and scent sticks.

- *Taste:* I am not a huge fan of oysters, but supposedly it has been proven by law that these puppies work sexual magic. I like using the oyster-on-the-half-shell concept by mixing warm chocolate with a blackberry brandy sauce and putting it in a candy shell that people can

What is that, velvet?

We all know what *this* dessert looks like. ANDREW BICKNELL PHOTOGRAPHY

toss back like a bivalve. Shared food, like fondue, or tasting menus that need to be passed among the guests also work well. These sharing rituals promote conversation and allow people to serve each other and interact. Offer food that won't make your guests look unattractive during the attack. If you're serving a white truffle sauce, which will be sure to get someone laid, pair it with a pasta that you don't have to twirl for ten years, like a penne or an easily cut pasta like papardelle. Don't serve smelly food with a ton of garlic or fishy fish. Display fruit that looks sexy—pomegranates, figs, passion fruit, kumquats, kiwis, mangoes. We all know what the banana signifies, so why not roll with it and flambé those beauties with caramelized brown sugar and port? Most people think the best aphrodisiac is alcohol. In proper doses it can be useful, but remember, kids—alcohol lasts longer on the shelf than it does in the bedroom.

MY FAVORITE DESIGN INSPIRATIONS

I love walking around New York City window-shopping at gorgeous stores like ABC Carpet & Home, Barneys, Moss, and Bergdorf Goodman. Their window displays do so much in such a small space. I also love looking at the fashions when autumn hits in New York—people put away their flip-flops and shorts and start rocking their fierce fall looks.

In places like Los Angeles, New Mexico, and Palm Springs, the landscape inspires me. I love the natural foliage, like desert succulents and wild bougainvillea. The dry desert has a different color palette—neutral tans mixed with the blues, lavenders, and deep oranges of the sunset, punched up with the lush greens of cacti and succulents.

In Europe, the architecture inspires me. That attention to

A few of my favorite things: my dog Hurricane, a bubble bath, and a glass of wine.
DAVID PFENDLER

detail in the ceilings, facades, or cobblestones in the sidewalks makes me always remember why the little things are so important.

I love simple flowers like daisies. Flowers have a natural beauty—they don't have to dress up or get boob jobs to look good. They also keep me on my toes because they are so perishable and fleeting.

I enjoy walking into restaurants filled with happy, socializing people, like Balthazar or Buddakan in New York, or The Edison Club in Los Angeles. I frequently steal ideas from these places for my parties, like the eighty-foot-tall Buddha statue from Tao or the horizontal chandelier from Town, both restaurants in New York.

I'm inspired by youth culture—what kids are wearing, how they deck out their cell phones, what they are listening to on their iPods, and so on.

My biggest inspirations are my clients. They tell me their dreams and I need to somehow express that in a digestible way for a roomful of people. This teaches me how to express their ideas, but also challenges me to add my own flair as well. So many times my clients wanted a certain look in a room that I never would have thought of. I may not have the same style, but it's great for me to stretch myself and be able to provide what they want in my own way.

Sometimes the best inspiration comes not from travel or fashion but from something that you hold dear,

like your grandmother's jewelry box. Nostalgia can be very inspiring.

● ● ●

So listen, I didn't forget about the ten-year-old girl—we're getting back to her. The point I want to make about her party's decor is that every facet of her event expressed her own personal style—no matter how sophisticated it was in the adult section or how playful it was in the kid section. We got to know this kid by asking her questions and looking around her bedroom to understand what her favorite things were, so the entire landscape illustrated *her* from the plush textures to the different shades of her favorite colors (pink and purple, natch) to the teddy-bear-shaped cookies at the end of the night. And that's all you need to do for your own party—ask yourself, what are your favorite things? What are the things that make you feel secure and energetic and happy? The answers can be anything:

freshly laundered white sheets, hearty Italian wines, exotic orchids, or French bulldogs. But make sure to use those answers to inform your design of a cohesive, remarkable space that will engage all the senses, all at once.

CHAPTER SEVEN

Music and Entertainment: Let's Get This Party Started!

There is a very good reason for the term *mood music*—music plays an integral part in determining the energy of an event. We once did a huge event for about a thousand lawyer guys over the age of sixty-five, and hoo-boy, I was at a total loss for the kind of entertainment we should provide at *that* party. The usual dance mixes would not fly here. In this case, we thought it would be best to turn the entertainment into a focal point instead of background noise, so we hired an emcee to host the entire event and double as a crooner who could perform the requisite Cole Porter tunes. We killed two birds with one stone, and found someone who was versatile enough to tackle the oldies as well as the newbies. The men were really tickled by some of the songs

from their era but also tolerated his smooth jazz versions of "Like a Virgin." It put them at ease; they felt comfortable with the songs they knew, and could also relate to the songs their children (or very young wives perhaps) listened to as well. As the evening wore on, the guests started tapping their feet and some even started dancing. And the emcee was phenomenal—cracking funny jokes but also staying appropriate with the crowd. In the middle of the party, we brought out a special performance by the Young at Heart Choir, which consists of a magnificent group of people age seventy-five and over who perform hard rock songs in choral arrangements. It was super charming to see these senior citizens rocking out to Def Leppard and Lynyrd

Skynyrd—the crowd loved it and felt young and carefree afterward.

Music can change the mood in the room just like lighting can. When serving dinner, turn it down a bit, along with the lights—maybe exchanging the dance hits for a sexy torch singer over candlelight. Since hearing is one of the five senses, every party should have a sound element, no matter how casual and last minute the get-together. For the big parties, you would hire a kick-ass sound engineer, a capable bandleader, or a DJ, but for smaller gigs, a varied **playlist** and a good stereo is all you really need.

PREPARING YOUR HOUSE FOR SOUND

Great audio should be heard on a consistent level from any point

These soft lounge-y beds filled with pillows and draping would suck up stray sound. JES GORDON

in your space. Audio is an art and should be installed by professionals, but if you are providing your own audio for a house party, be sure to test the levels from different zones in your home, including the stairwell and hard-surfaced rooms like kitchens and bathrooms. Make the environment thirsty for sound

by cushioning hard floors with area rugs and draping tiled or concrete walls. Any type of soft material, especially foam pillows, will suck up the sound so it doesn't bounce off the walls or floor. There is, however, too much of a good thing. If you bombard your space with soft, cushy sound magnets, your music will

end up in the Land of the Lost and you might be forced to entertain the troops on your own. Check your home for rooms that envelop sound and make it mushy and warped. Tiny rooms obviously get loud very quickly, but they are easier to manage than a large, cavernous one. If the levels are set correctly for a small, intimate space, it can be a wonderful environment for music.

You don't need to have forty-foot-tall speaker towers to have a good distribution of sound either. Most speakers on the market today, from small Bose CD players to larger systems, will get the job done, assuming you're not using a boom box from 1985. In terms of speaker innovations, one thing I like to promote for a house party are satellite speakers, which enable your guests to hear from anywhere in the venue. Satellite sound is a great option if your space has access to an outdoor area or rooftop—just wire up the satellite speakers anywhere you need music heard. That way, your guests do not feel as if they've completely left the party if they step outside.

Feel free to express yourself through the music you choose without it becoming a one-playlist evening. Share with your friends some cool music that makes you happy, but think of what everyone would like to hear. If you know for a fact that Great-Grandpa needs to hear some Dean Martin and the rest of your guests are twenty-three years old, maybe research some cool remakes of old tunes spiced up by DJs and play that instead.

MP3 players like iPods are very sexy little machines but, frankly, they should not become the focal point of your party. They should be hidden away so the obsessed iPod people don't hog the device all night, choosing their ultimate songs instead of socializing. I threw a house party for about eighty of my closest buddies, and I knew what would keep them moving for at least five hours. It was a high-energy

House parties rock! This is the moment we all strive for when compiling a playlist. ANDRE MAIER PHOTOGRAPHY

cocktail party, so I didn't rely too much on slow songs—just a few later in the night to signal the end of the party and to mellow people enough to get them the hell out of my house. I created a song list that was very long (like twenty hours for my five-hour party) so I wouldn't run out of tunes and set it to shuffle-and-repeat mode, so when the list did play out, it would rerun again in a refreshingly different order. But the most brilliant part of the evening was that my iPod was nowhere in sight. I used AirTunes, which is a program that works remotely from my iTunes program on my computer sending music to my stereo and speaker systems all over the house. People didn't know where the music was coming from, so they didn't even attempt to go and fiddle with

Who needs a DJ when you have a kick-ass stereo? DAVID PFENDLER

it. It was awesome! AirTunes can work through multiple speakers at once, so we were able to hear music through our stereo in the living room and through the TV in the den. I have to give full credit to my husband for this brilliance . . . guys dig hooking this stuff up.

If you want your evening to run as smooth as butter, and an iPod

is the only form of music you can afford, then I demand you designate a certain someone Master of the iPod. Go over with him or her your desired schedule of when you want certain songs to be played during the evening; that person can make sure your playlists don't run dry or can deal with any technical failures so you don't have to leave your guests

in a panic. (Take it from Jessica, who spent her wedding reception scrolling and clicking on her iPod in a back room because she hadn't edited the list correctly!) There is nothing worse than a party that goes completely silent—it's a real Debbie Downer. Electronics do have their glitches, so the best-case scenario is to make sure someone has another iPod on hand with a similar playlist. Another great feature on iTunes lets you play all your songs at the same level, so you don't have that mellow and cool moment followed by a terrifyingly loud song that blows everyone out of the room. This feature equalizes all your songs so they are played at the same level. If you're working with a stereo with an equalizer, it's always safe to make a smile pattern with the levels. Most of the time, this is a sure way to equalize the bass, treble, and other tones.

If you choose to go the old-school CD player route, that's cool—but once again you don't want a corner of your party to resemble a bunch of chicks at a sample sale. You need to designate someone to drive the CD player to make sure your evening doesn't hit those dreaded dead music zones—a multi-CD disc changer is ideal for this. Also burn CDs from your computer playlists for the mega mix from God, but don't forget that wonderful shuffle-and-repeat feature on your player.

Also, think outside the music box for home entertainment—your good old flat-screen television can play a part. I'm not suggesting letting folks sit back and watch old reruns of *The Jeffersons,* but looping a cool graphic movie could make for a nice background at a party. Once we did a swanky fashion event where we had a wall of TVs playing the Pamela Anderson and Tommy Lee sex tape over and over (What can I say, it was the times and it was a fashion party). We've projected movies into outdoor pools, so a Fellini flick is playing underwater while the guests snack on Italian cheeses and wine. You can project film and photo montages on any blank wall in any space for a great background visual at your event.

PUMP UP THE VOLUME (OR NOT)

Don't you hate it when you are at a party and you see a fella or chick you want to get with, you sidle over to chat, and the object of your attention can't hear a word you're saying? The perfect music volume allows normal conversation that is not too strained but has to be conducted at a slightly higher level. You want the music to be a presence at your event, but it shouldn't be a tyrant. There will always be audio **hot spots** where the volume is more intense and the focus is on the entertainment alone—like the **dance floor**—but there should always be safe havens from sound as well, like dining areas, bars, and outdoor terraces. People out there should still feel connected to the party but not in the eye of the storm. If you choose to have an impromptu performance by a solo artist like a saxophonist, put him or her in another hot spot, like a balcony that's visible to the whole party or the dance floor itself. After the performance is over, it's best to let your guests simmer down and recover, but don't let the room die either. Keep a steady stream of entertainment going, no matter what the level is. When I hire bands, I ask them for continual entertainment—some sort of action is required of them all evening. I'm not saying musicians aren't allowed to eat or pee, but if one of them leaves the stage, there should be a backup to keep the music flowing. When people first arrive at a party, it should be pumping—the music should be noticeable, but not so much that you can't say hello to people. If you're serving dinner, this is an obvious time to turn it down so people can converse. As the evening wears on and bellies get full, turn it up again; your guests might be antsy and looking for a reason to escape the person they've been trapped next to at the table!

SUGjesTION

Rocking Compilation CDs

- *The Funk Box* four-CD box set
- *A Night at the Playboy Mansion:* Dimitri from Paris
- *India: The Greatest Songs Ever*
- *Motown Remixed,* Volumes 1 and 2
- The *LateNightTales* series
- *Best of 80s Pop: Party Songs*
- *Jazzmatazz,* Volume 1
- *I Want My 80s* box set
- *California Soul: Rare Funk, Soul, Jazz, & Latin Grooves from the West Coast 1965–1981*
- Paul Oakenfold dance albums

Songs to Get Butts Moving

- "Celebrate"—Kool & the Gang
- "Flashlight"—Parliament
- "You & I"—Rick James
- "Borderline"—Madonna
- "Freeze Frame"—J. Geils Band
- "Dusic"—Brick
- "Upside Down"—Diana Ross
- "We Are Family"—Sister Sledge
- "Freak Out"—Chic
- "Superstition"—Stevie Wonder
- "Freedom"— George Michael
- "Come On Eileen"—Dexy's Midnight Runners
- "Dancing Machine"—Jackson 5
- "Gold Digger"—Kanye West
- "SexyBack"— Justin Timberlake
- "I Feel for You"—Chaka Khan

Every host of every party needs to watch the room like a security guard at a bank to make sure that no part of the party is robbing your guests of a good time. You may have a crowd that clearly came to get their groove on, so turn it up for them. If they start leaving, turn it down.

THEMED PARTY PLAYLISTS

For a **disco party** you can never go wrong with anything from ABBA, Chic, the BeeGees, early Michael Jackson, or Barry White. Just because it's a disco party doesn't mean that you should only play disco. You can have seventies R&B from Stevie Wonder and the Commodores and funk from Parliament. Some kick-ass hard rock groups will get your feet moving better than any hustle, like the Eagles, Heart, or Journey. Eighties songs like "Borderline" or "Holiday" by Madonna and Prince tunes are surefire winners, as well as some more current hits

by Justin Timberlake, Black Eyed Peas, or the Pussycat Dolls—or sample mash-up master Girl Talk for a mixture of every dance hit in one. You want to be sure to mix in a few slow tunes as well, just to give the evening some sort of break and give those of us who feel like fools a chance to grope someone on the dance floor.

For a **drunken brunch** I tend to go a little smooth with a nice acid jazz (like Gota's *It's So Different Here* or Ananda Project's *Release*) or dreamy like Air (I like Mark Ronson's *Alpha Beta Gaga* remix), Gorillaz, or the Chemical Brothers. I also like updated versions of old jazz tunes sung by modern artists such as Madeleine Peyroux, Jacqui Naylor, Amos Lee, Jamie Cullum, and the great Harry Connick Jr. Jacqui Naylor also takes pop songs from bands like U2 and the Talking Heads and jazzes them up. The *Verve Remixed* series of albums has jazz standards by the likes of Nina Simone, Billie Holiday, and Ella

If you're having a disco party, don't forget the ball.
WWW.HENSHALLPHOTOGRAPHY.COM

Fitzgerald reinterpreted by DJs through electronics—very hip.

At a **proper brunch** classical music, along the lines of Vivaldi's *Four Seasons,* is de rigueur to drink mimosas to. I play classical music at many of my daytime functions such as luncheons or teas. It's also great

That's me, enjoying a drunken brunch with my friends. JES GORDON

for shorter events like a baby shower or a book signing. If you want music with more octane than classical but with a subdued vibe, I like a fast-paced instrumental group like the Gypsy Kings or Béla Fleck.

With a **cocktail party** the drinks are flowing, the food is scarce—these things invariably turn into dime-size dance parties whether you want them to or not. (However, since cocktail parties traditionally run only two or three hours, it's easy to cut it off before

it gets too crazy.) Every cocktail party does well on some great DJ mixes by people like DJ Lars, DJ Shadow, DJ Lo, Faze Action (the *Moving Cities* album is awesome), Morcheeba's *Charango,* Dido (remixed), Zero 7's *Simple Things,* and Praful's *One Day Deep;* sexy crooners like Maxwell, Incognito, and the Brand New Heavies will keep the room energetic but mellow enough to socialize and hear important pickup lines. I like throwing in music that has an ethnic flair too. There are great DJ mixes with Indian or African influences or hip-shaking Latin grooves. The best way to become acquainted with new kinds of music is to whore around the iTunes store or Rhapsody and look under iMixes or compilations. (iMixes on iTunes are user generated, so you can get a huge range of stuff there.) Look around at music from other countries and languages, or find cool DJ remixes of Motown favorites like Smokey Robinson, Marvin Gaye, or Diana

Ross, or even eighties favorites like Prince and Michael Jackson.

HIRING A DJ

A client who was throwing a dance party for his twin teenage girls wanted them to have all the Hannah Montana and Jonas Brothers they needed to fuel the puberty party of a lifetime. He also invited one hundred and fifty adult guests who were family members, friends, and business associates. This event was to be about seven hours long—so the best way to ensure a large, varied music playlist was to hire a DJ. Usually DJs are current with today's music scene for all ages, and their talent lies in presenting these tunes in a consistent, endless flow, sometimes with their own remixes added to the mix. DJs also work on their own so it's easier for them to move with the ebb and flow of the party, changing their tunes to match the mood. The DJ can also double as an emcee for the evening, making announcements and keeping

Songs for Lovin'

- "Deep Waters"—Incognito
- "You're the Best Thing"—The Style Council
- "Slave to Love"—Bryan Ferry and Roxy Music
- "Hands of Time"—Groove Armada
- "Trouble"—Ray LaMontagne
- "Lovely Day"—Bill Withers
- "Two Fine People"—Cat Stevens
- "Undress Me Now"—Morcheeba
- "Follow You Follow Me"—Phil Collins
- "In Your Eyes"—Peter Gabriel
- "Someone Like You"—Van Morrison or Dina Carroll
- "You Make My Dreams Come True"—Hall and Oates
- "Stay"—Chaka Khan
- "Maybe"—k.d. lang
- "One of These Things First"—Nick Drake
- "Ascension"—Maxwell
- "A Song for You"—Herbie Hancock, featuring Christina Aguilera
- "Sittin' in the Middle"—Raul Midon
- "One Love"—U2, featuring Mary J. Blige

- "Don't Wait Too Long"—Madeleine Peyroux
- "Hopeless"—Dionne Ferris
- "Honeysuckle Rose"—Jane Monheit
- "A Lot Like Love"—Aqualung
- "Ordinary People"—John Legend
- "You'll Never Find Another Love Like Mine"—Lou Rawls
- "I Believe (When I Fall in Love with You)"—Stevie Wonder
- "Love TKO"—Teddy Pendergrass
- "Killing Me Softly"—Roberta Flack
- and of course the king of romance—*anything* by Barry White!

We used a scrim to hide the DJ's booth at this fashion party.
ANDRE MAIER PHOTOGRAPHY

things moving. The emcee factor can mean the possibility for serious cheesiness, though, so I'd suggest checking out the banter beforehand at a live show to see how the DJ candidate rolls. Remember, you may adore a DJ at your favorite club, but that individual may not be so hot as an event DJ; just because DJs can get folks hopping on a crowded dance floor doesn't mean they will understand there are appropriate (and inappropriate) times to play certain types of music at an event. The best DJs are super tech savvy—up on all the latest equipment, like video screens of moving images that correlate to the music they are spinning. Great places to find event DJs are event Web sites like totalentertainment .com or cityconnection.com, but Googling for those in your area is best. Make sure you ask for a sample of their work. Usually, they'll have a MySpace page with samples, or a

demo CD you can listen to. The best way is to watch them work another party. If you're renting a venue, the staff can recommend DJs they've worked with well in the past.

DJ services range in price, big time: Some start at $1,500 to $7,500, not including turntables and fancy setups (many DJs will want to rent sound equipment at the location instead of lugging it around themselves). Then you have your world-famous club and fashion show DJs who get as much as $20,000 to $50,000 a gig, stay in the finest hotels, and travel first class as part of their deals. Some DJs fit into special ethnic niches, such as Greek and Indian performers who understand the specific traditions that Greek or Indian celebrations would need to follow. I personally like mixing technology with real musicians, and a great compromise for this is to hire a DJ *and* a kickin' horn section or percussionist to play alongside. This adds a great live element to the evening, so it's not so canned.

HIRING A LIVE BAND

Don't tell anyone, but having an amazing band at your event is the best thing the world of entertaining can offer. If the band is so good that your guests can't sit down, they won't notice that the food isn't that great or that the centerpiece is dead. Although you don't want the band to overshadow everything once you've slapped down cash for all the other details, having an awesome band is a built-in **wow factor** that people will talk about long after the party's over.

I come from a family of musicians, so I am allowed to say that they can sometimes be an interesting bunch. If you've decided to hire a rock band you love that has never played an event, the musicians may not know that it's not cool to show up half in the bag or that they shouldn't be pinching your sixteen-year-old daughter's ass. We once hired a band we saw playing in a club—one of the most exciting musical experiences I have ever had. We were with our clients at the time and they simply *had* to have this band play at their twenty-fifth anniversary party. So we approached the band members to play the gig, and for an enormous sum (like $50,000, to be exact), they said yes. Unfortunately, they neglected to tell us that they had a **technical rider** longer than the Bible that included some sort of orange soda I had never heard of, cocaine, hookers, and Tootsie Rolls. These additional caveats spiked the bill to $100K so, needless to say, the wife didn't get those teardrop diamond earrings she'd been wanting her whole married life. The point I am trying to make is that when hiring the band, it can't only be about the band—it has to be about the client and the guests and what makes *them* happy. Even though these guys might think they are rock stars, they need to make the client happy, and that means playing well, showing up on time, dressing appropriately, staying sober, and being professional like any other vendor. Just because they are creative or artsy doesn't give them license to be unprofessional in any way.

A great event band will have promotional material you can watch, like a demo DVD that shows their range of songs and performing style. Sometimes you can get a multiple act in the deal—a string section or acoustic guitarist who can peel off from the larger band and play for a quieter cocktail hour, for instance, or a horn section that can move into the crowd. Some bands will have an in-house DJ who can play the **after party** for those who want to keep raging. Try to sample local bands at a showcase night at a club so you can actually see them in action. Even if your party has nothing to do with nuptials, log onto wedding Web sites like theknot.com for some good local suggestions. Peruse your newspaper for live music acts—most bands have to do events in order to stay afloat. However, make sure the band knows event-speak: how to run an

Will the artists be bringing their own sound equipment to the party? Make sure you cover that in the contract. ANDRE MAIER PHOTOGRAPHY

evening that may include **toasts** and/ or announcements, special dances

(like the Hora at a Jewish wedding, for instance), when to quiet down during meal time, and when to get the room moving again.

THE ABCS OF BAND CONTRACTS

1. **Attire**: Your band needs to dress well, usually in something similar and monochromatic like black suits and ties. Female torch singers need to look gorgeous but not slutty—dresses that cover up their naughty bits are a must. If the party is more casual, some people like the band to reflect that by wearing something funky or rock and roll, but you should always discuss the desired attire at hiring time. You don't want a room full of people in black tie listening to a band in ripped jeans.

2. The band should provide you with a song list of its repertoire—you should also be

able to request songs that aren't on the list, within reason.

3. Specify those times in the evening when you expect the band to do something, whether it's making an announcement or performing a certain song.

4. The contract should state whether meals are expected during contract time, and whether the contracted time includes travel and equipment setup.

5. The contract should be clear about who exactly will be playing in the band. Often bands switch members for simultaneous gigs somewhere else, so make sure the people playing at your event will be the band you fell in love with.

6. Ask if the contract includes sound equipment like **monitor speakers,** transportation,

someone to set them up and break them down, and possibly a sound engineer who works a sound board.

7. Do the musicians require staging or do they bring their own props? It's important to know if you have to spend mucho bucks to just set up the band before the music even starts.

8. Will the band provide continual sound or a system that will play when the group leaves the stage for breaks? It's rotten when the players need to take a leak and the room goes dead. They either need to have musicians who remain on the stage and break in turns, or a backup sound system that plays music while they are gone.

9. What are the power needs for the equipment? Can your venue or home handle it, or will you have to rent a generator?

Hiring a band is a big commitment but can be very well worth it. Pricing for bands really varies. Professional event bands that have nine pieces or more tend to range anywhere from $5,000 to $45,000, depending on where you live and what you expect from them. Local smaller bar bands probably range from about $1,500 to $5,000, depending on their size. We once hired a band from a music school nearby—it was amazing, and the musicians only requested a meal and car fare for their payment. You gotta love that!

TESTES, TESTES, ONE, TWO: MICROPHONES

When your 101-year-old great-grandfather has braved every staircase in town to make it to your event, you really want his toast to be heard. For that, there is a world of amazing microphones out there. If you have hired professional musicians, they can provide the microphone and control sound

levels. In other cases, handheld wireless mics seem to be the most popular choice—people like to hold something when they are nervous, and they won't trip over the cord. Some microphones are as small as ladybugs and pin onto your lapel. All of these mics are available to rent from a local audio/visual provider or to purchase in electronic stores like Radio Shack and Best Buy. Make sure to test the sound beforehand and to coach anyone making a speech on how to hold a mic properly so your guests aren't subject to that nails-on-a-chalkboard screech. An ideal distance from mouth to microphone is three to four inches.

THINKING OUTSIDE THE ROCK BOX

You don't need to hire the typical rock and roll band (or jazz combo or string quartet) for your party—this is a great time to get creative as a party planner. I like the juxtaposition of modernizing

Ethnic flavor is another way to expand your horizons. Instead of your average string quartet playing Pachelbel's Canon in D for your sophisticated brunch, provide a flamenco guitarist or sitar player to play the tune instead. A line of Brazilian drummers at the entrance to your party will get the mood hopping as soon as your guests arrive.

It might just be me, but I love chorus singers too. Whether they hail from your church, high school, women's club, or barbershop, the array of voices is such a treat to listen to. When a chorus is beautifully trained, there is nothing like it.

FROM FORTUNE-TELLERS TO FIRE-EATERS

It's a good idea to change the entertainment during the evening to wake up your guests. Once everyone has gotten a little groove on and settled down, it's fun to throw a short-term act into the mix. We once staged an impromptu acrobatic

You don't have to choose just one—mix up a live pianist with a DJ for something truly unique. WWW.HENSHALLPHOTOGRAPHY.COM

classical instruments, like a harp or violin, by making them electric. We once hired a harpist who played electric rock and roll and it was so cool—eerie and ethereal, all coming from this conservative lady sitting at this conservative instrument. I've also added an electric violin to a rock and roll cover band, which made it so eclectic and interesting. Or introduce your guests to more unusual instruments, like accordions or xylophones. Adding them to the mix creates an element of surprise and gives your party's entertainment some wow factor.

The best music will appeal to every generation at your party, from young to old. ANDRE MAIER PHOTOGRAPHY

performance with Cirque du Soleil members dropping from the ceiling while the event was in full swing! It was very exciting and even a bit scary, but people loved the twist in the evening.

Or add some little moments of kitsch, like cigarette girls passing out candy cigarettes, roaming fortune-tellers, go-go dancing girls (or boys), fire-eaters, jugglers, or random people walking around on

Songs (and Albums) to Mellow Out the Crowd

- "San Paolo"—Morcheeba
- "Ain't No Sunshine"—Bill Withers
- "Wild and Peaceful"—Incognito
- "When I Lose My Way"—Randy Crawford
- "These Are The Days"—Jamie Cullum
- "Why"—Annie Lennox
- *Graceland*—Paul Simon
- *Tje Ni Mousso*—Amadou & Mariam
- *The Color Five*—Jacqui Naylor
- *All You Can Eat*—k.d. lang

- *Maxwell's Urban Hang Suite*—Maxwell
- *Down to the Moon*—Andreas Vollenweider
- "Grass"—XTC
- *Brother Sister*—The Brand New Heavies
- "In the Hand of the Inevitable"—James Taylor Quartet
- *Moon Safari*—Air
- *Freedom Flight*—Shuggie Otis

stilts. Get artistic with photo booths set up with real photographers, henna tattoo artists, airbrush artists, karaoke stations, or glassblowers. I love this stuff because it's so much fun—but too much fun can get annoying. I don't want a fortune-teller up my ass while I am trying to wolf down some carbs at the buffet, so these types of specialty entertainers should be limited to mobile parts of your party like a cocktail hour, or toward the middle of the evening when folks are getting slightly bored. These entertainers don't need to hang out all night but rather come in and out of a party when it needs a jolt.

Talent agencies out there handle all sorts of entertainment through one company. For one very busy bat mitzvah, we used one company to provide video games for kids, motivational dancers, a DJ with two sax players, a hypnotist, a tattoo artist, an airbrush artist, a strolling fortune-teller, an R & B band for the cocktail hour, and a rock and roll band for later in the evening. Obviously, you can choose bits and pieces for smaller-scale parties, but mixing it up is a great way to avoid having too many rock stars in the kitchen for one event.

Miscellaneous entertainers hired through a talent agency will probably charge you hourly per act with a certain number of hours minimum. Most of the time it's a three- to five-hour minimum, which you can spread out throughout the event, including travel time and a meal on site for them as well. They should be responsible for their own costumes and whatever other props they need. Most independent entertainers charge $150 to $1,500 per hour, depending on what they do. Add to that price any extra materials like photo printing or T-shirts for airbrushing stations.

You will probably need to provide a dressing area—a place for the entertainers to stash their personal belongings and get organized. It's also nice to designate someone to oversee the entertainers in case they have any needs or get lost on the way.

• ● •

You don't have to go with a gazillion forms of music and entertainment, just do what works best for your event—even if it's just firing up your iPod or hiring a dude in a Barney costume for a few hours!

CHAPTER EIGHT

Food and Drink: The *Real* Reason Everyone Shows Up at Your Party

Where do people gather at gatherings? At the bar, around the buffet, in the kitchen—all the places where they can get their greedy little hands on some grub. I may not be consciously hungry when I arrive at a party, but, nevertheless, I first need to know where the bar is and where the hell the food is coming from to feel at home. It's not only a physical need to be fed and watered—it's a psychological need. When you first arrive at a party (sober of course), there is an obvious state of awkwardness. What do you do? Whom do you talk to? So you grab a drink and a bite of food so you have something to do with your mouth and your hands. But it's not just that. Good food makes you feel provided for, its warmth comforts, and its flavors open up your senses to your environment. It also offers a balancing counterpoint to drinks, which provide the springboard for conversation and socialization. It takes away the party jitters and evens out some of the rough edges. Your dress may be too tight or your hair slightly askew, but after you've had that first sip of champagne, you feel like Grace Kelly. There is a fine line between feeling like Grace Kelly and acting like Courtney Love, though, so make sure you moderately indulge in this social lubricant.

In this chapter you'll find out how to stock a comprehensive (but not costly) home bar, and whip up a smart cocktail and serve it up in style. I'll also teach hosts how to whet the appetites of their guests with simple, sophisticated food from the country's best chefs, such as Glenn Harris and Jeffrey Lefcourt (owners of Jane, The Smith, and The Neptune Room, all in New York), Heathe St. Clair (of The Sunburnt Cow and Bondi Road in New York), and some of my favorite catering chefs on this planet, such as Suzanne Gilliam from New York's The Catering Company and Andrea Baumgardner from Green Market Catering in Fargo, North Dakota, plus their creative menu ideas for classic cocktail parties, holiday feasts, football parties, and everything in between.

GETTING YOUR DRINK ON: SETTING UP A HOME BAR

When hosting an event, you don't want your guests wanting what you *don't* have, but you also don't want to line the walls with every alcohol known to man—that only leads to major trouble. A client of caterer Suzanne Gilliam once told her, "Well, my guests can certainly have whatever they'd like to drink, but what *I'm* offering is this." I love this attitude. As a host, you need to be comfortable not offering the world of alcohols and confident in your edited selections. For a cocktail party, it makes sense to offer one signature cocktail, a few mixers like vodka and gin with juice or tonic, a couple of wine selections, a couple of beer choices, and a scotch or whiskey—that will definitely cover your bases. A dinner party should be complete with wine choices, plus perhaps an after-dinner drink like port or a digestif. A luncheon just needs a punch or wine, sparkling water, and coffee and tea.

ESSENTIAL BAR TOOLS

Corkscrew

I especially like the Metrokane Rabbit Lever Style Corkscrew ($60). I don't know how it works,

but somehow it's way easier than all the rest of the cork pullers out there. The waiter-style pulltap corkscrew is a cheaper option that also works very well once you get the hang of it.

Ice Bucket

You need buckets for chilling beer and wine bottles, and also buckets to hold your drinking ice (these should be separate, obviously). Choose something relatively shallow so when it comes time to dump out the old stuff, you don't need to visit a chiropractor afterward.

Ice Scoop

Since you really don't want your guests sticking their fingers in your ice bucket, an ice scoop is a must. If you have a steady hand, go for the fancier ice tongs!

Cocktail Shaker/Strainer

Not only is this tool festive and great for those flabby upper arms, it gets you one step closer to that dream of becoming a professional mixologist.

Every drink seems cooler when it's been shaken first. Make sure you measure with a **jigger.**

Colander

A good old pasta colander is great for avoiding those sink clogs from lemon or lime rinds. Keep a strainer over the sink drain to avoid having a plumber become one of your party guests.

Wine Buckets

These are great to have at a dinner party to keep your whites chilled. Wine buckets come in a self-standing style so you don't have to waste precious table space, or you can incorporate one into your tabletop design if you have the room. Cool varieties come in marble, chrome, Lucite, or glass.

Wine Stoppers

It's important to let your wine breathe but not hyperventilate. At some point you need to close that puppy up so it will last if you don't finish the bottle (as if!). Check out kitchenware stores like Sur la Table and Williams-Sonoma for pretty examples.

Decanters

If you don't feel like showing off the label of your wine at your party or if you are serving a big red that needs lots of oxygen action, then simply relocate the wine to a glass decanter. The wide base lets the wine breathe and the flavor deepen.

Garnishes

While you don't need to have every one of the following things on hand, it's helpful to have your garnishes precut and ready to go when mixing up your guests' drinks.

- bitters
- citrus (lemon, lime, and orange)
- coarse salt
- cocktail onions
- hot pepper sauce
- Maraschino cherries
- olives
- simple syrup
- Worcestershire

In terms of the physical setup, you should always display the evening's selection for the guests so you don't have to explain over and over what's available. I usually take one bottle of each kind of beer or wine and put it on top of the bar; if I'm doing a signature cocktail, I'll type up a description and put it in a cool picture frame on the bar or write it in chalk on a mini blackboard. At a recent cocktail party, I came up with a drink called Good Times—ginger beer, limoncello, and vodka with a garnish of candied ginger served in a stemless martini glass—and I just put that description in a Lucite frame so my guests could request it by name. If you are lucky enough to have hired a bartender for the evening, they often set up a **back bar** behind the bar for the rest of the necessities—and you should do the same if you're bartending to keep your service space clean and uncluttered. Keep your chilled items on **ice** behind you, and service towels on hand to deal with any drips.

Skewered blackberries, crystalized ginger, and citrus wedges liven up a boring cocktail. THE CATERING COMPANY

Where should you get your drinks for the party? Personally, I've been buying alcohol (long before it was legal for me to do so) at Astor Wines in New York. They have an awesome Web site (astorwines.com) too. Wine.com is also a good online resource for buying booze or just researching before you head to the store.

If you're buying in bulk for a party, Trader Joe's has amazingly cheap wine offerings—although I'd caution against the Two-Buck Chuck category of wine as it'll fell your guests with killer migraines and gut rot. I've heard you can get incredible deals on "Easter eggs" at Costco—special hidden gems at remarkable prices—and their Kirkland brand of wines are surprisingly tasty. (Although you might want to hide the bottles from your guests!)

If you go to a local wine store or liquor retailer, most will offer discounts on cases—even mixed cases. Also, by going to a smaller store, you may have the opportunity to taste some selections before choosing—not something mega stores like Costco offer.

And last, how much should you buy? Basically, one bottle of wine should provide four to six glasses; for hard alcohol, you should have about twenty-two to twenty-five servings per liter. I usually multiply my number of guests by four—meaning if I had ten guests, I would have forty bottles of beer (on the wall). And as I said in chapter 2, at some stores, you can buy alcohol based on consumption and return any unopened bottles for store credit or cash. Long story short, it's better to have too much than too little. And keep the day of the week in mind; Saturday nights are known for much heavier drinking, since guests know they have that lazy Sunday to sleep it off. So if your party is a Saturday Night Special, pad your supply!

WINES: VIVA VINO!

Some type of wine choice is a must at most parties. Ever since the movie *Sideways,* wine tasting seems to be a sexy and fun hobby—your local wine stores probably hold tastings or educational classes right on the premises. People who know a lot about wine are very passionate about the subject and will go to major lengths to help you find the drink of your dreams. Once again, wine preference is such a personal thing that you need to taste it yourself find out what you like and what you don't. It's a tough job, but somebody's gotta do it.

For the average cocktail hour before a dinner party, I think it's fine to offer one red and one white variety, and if you feel that your guests will go for it, then one rosé too. I serve more inexpensive wines at a cocktail hour (like under $10 a bottle) so I can save my budget for the dining experience, but that's up to you. There are some incredible cheap wines out there that consistently get top reviews at my parties. My husband and I discovered an awesome Italian brand, Voga, by falling in love with its ultramodern bottle (reminiscent of a Voss water bottle) that comes with a cork and a screw top, which comes in handy if you want to drink the rest later after the cork has been popped. Very cool looking—and we actually liked the taste of the merlot and pinot grigio they offer. Another priceworthy brand I like is Bogle Vineyards, which comes in several varietals. Both of these brands run around $8 a bottle.

There are loads of wine values out there, and the best way to get them is to focus on the secondary wine regions, like Germany, Austria, Spain, Italy, Australia, and New Zealand. If you're only looking at the benchmark wine regions, like Bordeaux, Burgundy, or super Tuscan, it's going to cost you more.

I've also served Japanese sake at many cocktail parties, and people loved it! The higher-end sakes don't need to be warmed but can be chilled like a white wine. There are so many different designations of sake, I won't get into it here—but definitely go to a knowledgeable liquor store that stocks sake and ask for recommendations.

Once again, I feel that safe glassware is best at any event, meaning ones without stems. You can use an ice bucket for your white wines, but be sure you have a service napkin ready to cradle that dripping baby when you pull it out of the ice. Otherwise you can use those individual cooler cozies for bottles that stay dry.

Sparklers

Champagne conjures up glamorous images of supermodels in skinny black dresses, so it's always on the party list, particularly for the womenfolk. Champagne also seems to be accepted as one of the food groups, often used as a hunger management device for those of us who need to wear Spanx under our dresses. (It's the bubbles—they fill up your tummy.) And it's always acceptable to offer a more cost-effective option like Prosecco or another sparkling wine from the United States or Spain (cavas have great value for the taste). Most Americans can't tell the difference between a fine sparkling and your average champagne, and if you're making punch from champagne, all the more reason to go for the non-French sparklers. Personal "poppers" are fun—mini bottles of champagne (187 ml) served with a straw to get those bubbles up into that brain area as quickly as possible. Pommery Pop is the most notable, but Sofia Coppola makes a blanc de blancs in a very pretty red can too.

Here are some of my fizzy favorites, from bling to bargain basement:

- Vilmart Grand Cellier d'Or Brut, 2001 ($75)
- Marc Hebrart, Rosé Brut ($42)
- Veuve Clicquot Brut ($40)
- Gloria Ferrer Sonoma Brut ($15)
- Prosecco Brut, Col Vetoraz ($16)
- Prosecco Frozza ($13)
- Freixenet Cordon Negro ($15)
- Korbel Blanc de Noirs ($12)
- Codorniu Napa Brut Cava Classico ($11)

I love being a glassware rebel and serving champagne in a highball glass instead of a flute. Flutes are wonderfully sexy and charming, and the narrow aperture supposedly encourages sipping, but dainty glassware is a danger to all. High-stemmed glasses that can be knocked down easily just make me nervous. The only time I would feel safe having stemmed glassware would be at a dinner party where people were practically nailed to their chairs . . . although passing the peas could even cause trouble. I want my guests to feel carefree when celebrating with me, not cautious. Therefore, I'm a fan of using tall and slender drink glasses that I fill about a quarter of the way up.

Whites

You can get away with a cheaper white if it's served very cold, and every host loves white wine at parties since it's not so scary to spill. One of my very favorite pinot grigios is from the Italian maker, Santa Margherita, which you can find for around $20. Some other good options:

- Kim Crawford Sauvignon Blanc ($16)
- Pacific Rim Reisling ($10)
- Berger Grüner Veltliner ($13)
- Louis Jadot Mâcon Villages ($13)
- Juan de Alzate Rioja Blanco ($12)

Reds

It's a little harder to cheat with red wine—the übercheap options will give you an insta-headache or they taste like cough syrup. If you're serving a red at a dinner party, you don't want to blast people's taste buds with a big, heavy cabernet that will conflict with the meal and make your guests feel sedated. Instead, go for a well-balanced, berry-focused, medium-bodied pick, like a California zinfandel. Again, your best bet is to go to a local wine shop and ask the pros for their recommendations of a priceworthy, easily drinkable, food-friendly red.

If I'm serving an Italian white, like a pinot grigio, I like to complement it with a Trabucchi Valpolicella, which is about $18 per bottle. I love Italian reds, like Chianti Classico; also check out Lomazzi & Sarli's organic Negroamaro Giràle, $10. I had a mind-blowing experience recently with a chilled bubbly red called Penisola Sorrentina Gragnano Monteleone ($14). Usually reds conjure a more wintry image in my head, but this red was quite refreshing and fizzy—a nice option for a summer soiree, perhaps. Here are a few other reds that are good bets:

- Perrin Réserve Côtes-du-Rhône ($10)
- Bodegas Borsao Crianza Seleccion ($15)
- Marques de Caceres Rioja Crianza ($13)
- Big House Red ($10)
- Domaine du Vissoux Beaujolais ($15)

Pinks

Rosés are no longer the cheesy white zinfandel bastard cousin of wine—

Unless you're throwing a frat party, offer some imported brewskies.
WWW.HENSHALLPHOTOGRAPHY.COM

many dry rosés have flooded the market and are perfect for summer parties and luncheons. Just make sure the pink wine you purchase is not sweet—think South of France, not Boone's Farm Strawberry. I have never been disappointed with the Tavel Côtes du Rhône Rosé Domaine Pélaquié 2007, priced at about $16 per bottle. More rosé recommendations:

- Bonny Doon Vin Gris de Cigare ($15)
- Castello di Ama Rosato ($16)
- Bodegas Muga Rosado ($11)
- Domaine de Fontsainte Corbières Gris de Gris ($14)
- Robert Sinskey Vin Gris ($20)

Beer

Males at parties are always in dire need of beer. Public drinking seems to bring out the testosterone in men; it's like a guy needs to be seen with a beer or whiskey in his hand in front of the other guys, not a green appletini. To avoid turning your event into a frat party, offer up some microbrews or a stronger European style, like a German pilsner or wheat beer (which can be garnished with a lemon wedge). Couple the beer with some yummy food—we've done warm soft pretzels passed on a tray with mini glasses of dark ale. It's also great to support a local brewery at your event. In New York we often serve Brooklyn Lager; in New Orleans it's Abita. In most cases, kegs really shouldn't be at an upscale event—beer should be served in attractive, chilled glassware, if possible, or at the very least, in chilled bottles.

COCKTAILS: BEYOND THE COSMO

When we were teenagers, we sucked down anything in a bottle just to get a buzz. As we grow older, our tastes start to settle down a little. The thought of a strawberry wine cooler from 7-Eleven would now put my tummy in a tailspin, but the thought of a great sangria with fresh fruit would rock my world—and that's basically a wine cooler for grown-ups. (Hey, maybe I have grown up . . .) Mixed drinks for the grown-up crowd have evolved from the Mountain Dew and vodka mixtures of your youth,

The Moo-Mosa

This creative signature cocktail is from one of my favorite watering holes in New York, The Sunburnt Cow (courtesy of Heathe St. Clair, chef and owner).

Combine equal parts:

- sake
- sparkling wine
- orange juice

Serve chilled. To mix things up, you can infuse the sake with different fruits and change your juices accordingly.

Pineapple and Mango Sake

- 2 gallons sake
- 2 mangoes
- 1 pineapple

Peel and chop fruit, add to sake and let sit for a day or two. Cheers!

and they can be a fun addition to your entertaining playbook.

If you're having a cocktail party (or any kind of party, really), offering your guests a signature cocktail is classy and very celebratory. It doesn't have to be anything insane requiring Tom-Cruise-in-*Cocktail*-level bartending skills—just a favorite cocktail, like a sangria or mojito, jazzed up with special, seasonal flavors. Add ginger to a mojito, a champagne punch for an Asian-themed party, put pear nectar in champagne punch for a Thanksgiving dinner, and add watermelon to your summer margarita.

THE STAPLES: VODKA, GIN, WHISKEY, RUM, AND TEQUILA

The chicks will most likely hit your vodka supply (it's low in carbs and can be mixed with lots of pretty colored liquids). But don't discount vodka as a lightweight—it's also easily perked up with festive seasonal mixers such as fresh

pomegranate juice, passion fruit juice, or even a light pumpkin puree in the fall months. I usually just buy a good pure potato vodka like Monopolowa—it might not have the sex appeal of the other brands, but it's very good. I love Belvedere vodka too; it makes me feel like Julie Christie in *Dr. Zhivago* wearing a gorgeous fur hat, gliding through mounds of snow on a horse-driven carriage. Flavored vodkas, like blackberry, vanilla, peach, and pepper, are great for parties too, since many can hold a drink on their own by just adding ice and a splash of something else—pure simplicity. A college friend turned me on to a green-tea-flavored vodka from a brand called Charbay; mix with ginger beer and lime, and you've got one hell of a smooth drink on your hands. Try flavored vodka with squeezed lemon or lime and soda water, pomegranate juice, cranberry juice, tomato juice, or grapefruit juice. Vodka is the baseline for every martini known to man: the dirty

martini, the chocolate martini, the saketini, the lychee martini . . . the list is endless, as are guests' appetites for these kinds of drinks.

But vodka isn't the only buzz game in town. Gin, whiskey, and rum are easily married to mixers to create some stellar party drink options. Gin gets kind of a bad rap as an old person's drink since it's rarely advertised with leggy blondes or rap stars—gin's vibe is more about grassy tennis courts and top hats. Gin is usually interchangeable with vodka, like in martinis; you're either for one team or the other it seems. Gin is great for summery drinks, like refreshing gin and tonics, Tom Collins, and gimlets. Tanqueray Ten is a nice herbaceous gin, as is Hendricks. Whiskey drinks are also sort of old-timey—think old-fashioneds, mint juleps, and Manhattans—but those cocktails are coming back in style. Jim Beam Green Label, Early Times, and good old Jack Daniels work well for these kinds of drinks, as do Irish whiskeys like Jameson. Then there is the Devil Incarnate: tequila. For making margaritas, I like inexpensive choices like Sauza Silver and José Cuervo Gold. For sipping, there's Patron Silver for slightly more pesos. With rum on hand, you have the world of fun tropical drinks to employ—mai tais, mojitos, Cuba libres, piña coladas, planter's punch, and daiquiris. Some rums I like: Ron Abuelo Anejo, Mount Gay Eclipse Silver, and simply, Bacardi Select.

Now for cocktail glassware. The silhouette of a martini glass is as sexy as Heidi Klum in her skivvies, but damn they are dangerous and usually not worth the trouble. Stemless glassware has hit the market big time, so you should have no trouble finding stemless martini glasses at places like Sur la Table and Bed Bath & Beyond. Some may frown upon serving an old-school cocktail in a differently styled glass, but I say so be it. If I can avoid cleaning up my house for weeks after a party, I am willing to hazard their disapproval.

SCOTCH

If you are hosting a mixed-bag crowd, it is important to offer stuff for every age group—older gentlemen prefer a good glass of scotch to nurse throughout the evening. Not all of us can afford to go the twenty-five-year-old Glenlivet route; Clan MacGregor, Ballantine's, or Johnny Walker Red are more wallet friendly.

AFTER-DINNER DRINKS

I don't know if these drinks truly help with digestion, but they are certainly festive. After-dinner drinks like port and sambuca seem popular at most events, along with coffee or even spiced coffee with a shot of Kahlúa or Bailey's to accompany it. Sweet dessert wines should be sipped in small quantities, like the end-of-the-night treat they are. I suggest using small, narrow glasses for these wines to encourage moderation. Two dessert wine picks to try: Telmo Rodríguez Málaga MR Moscatel ($16) and G. D. Vajra Moscato d'Asti ($20). For port, I

like to serve Duck Walk Blueberry Port ($16)—this stuff is so delicious, I sometimes pour it over vanilla ice cream and call it a night!

The one time I propose using stemmed glasses is for drinks like cognac or brandy—but short stems only. I love those big globes that take in your entire face in one sip. These feel pretty sturdy to me and I love what they signify: the end of the evening where we are content, full, and sleepy.

NONALCOHOLIC LIBATIONS

For those who prefer not to partake, try to make the nonalcoholic choices just as glamorous by presenting them in fabulous glassware and infusing them with good fruit juice as you would any cocktail. Any guest can take part in a champagne toast with a high-end sparkling cider like Martinelli's; Trader Joe's has some great sparkling juices as well in pomegranate, white grape, or blueberry flavors. Or toast with fruit-

If there's drinking at your party, make sure to set up little bowls of nibbles, like nuts, popcorn, and crackers. ANDRE MAIER PHOTOGRAPHY

infused sparkling water—just let fresh blackberries (or whatever you like) steep in some bubbly water for a while before the party starts.

If kids are invited, make sure to include them in the fun too. There is nothing wrong with keeping a supply of juice boxes under your bar to avoid any glass breakage or an ice-cube-choking episode. If kids request soda, keep noncaffeinated options on hand and attractive hard plastic cups to serve it in. If you have the time and June Cleaver inclination, it's awesome to offer your little guests a variety of egg creams and milk shakes to keep them occupied and sugar smacked.

OPEN BARS AT VENUES

Most venues charge people a certain rate for certain amount of time; some will then charge for consumption for the last hour or so. Most venues would agree to offering a limited bar to keep costs down. Before renting a space and agreeing on an open bar, you need to understand what the bar costs include since it's different at every venue. Does it include non-alcoholic beverages like soft drinks, juices, and mixers? Bar fruit and condiments? Bartenders and bar backs? Glassware or only plastics? Ask your contact at the venue to be specific.

To be perfectly honest, I have *never* had a cash bar at any of my events. I feel that if you are hosting an evening, you need to provide everything for your guests—unless it's for a charity and the proceeds are going somewhere virtuous.

FOOD: FROM NUTS TO SOUP

This is obviously a huge topic, so let's start out small—cocktail nibbles. Even when your party is mainly a booze party, you still have to provide something for your guests to munch on or you're going to have a lot of inebriated jackasses in your house. It's important to scatter a few platters and bowls around the room so people don't huddle around the only chip-and-dip platter.

First, the ubiquitous bowl of nuts. When I hear the word *almonds,* the first thing I think of are those dreadful pastel candy-coated wedding favors. Why waste calories on those things when there are so many other great options available? Almonds aren't the be-all and end-all in the world of snack nuts, but they are more cost-effective than macadamias, more exotic than peanuts, and they don't make you wrestle with a shell for fifteen minutes like pistachios. Almonds are healthy, meaty little animals, so why not mess up all that good nutrition by encrusting them with ingredients like melted butter, brown sugar, and cinnamon for a sweet kick? Or go a spicier

route and dust the almonds with a little chili powder—it'll keep your guests thirsty and your bartenders busy. Purists can roast their own raw almonds in olive oil and sea salt (but remember to use very little oil, like a teaspoon for a couple of cups of nuts). Heat them at 350 degrees for about ten minutes until they start smelling good and darkening a little. Toast pecan halves the same way, and while they're in the oven, mix cayenne, brown sugar, sea salt, and rosemary with a little melted butter. Toss the warm ingredients with the warm pecans and then heat in the oven for another minute so the spice mixture sticks. If you're having a Mexican fiesta, toss peanuts with some lime juice, chili powder, cumin, and salt. The possibilities are endless, but just don't forget the salt when making your own mixed-nuts recipe—that's the most important part.

Heaping bowls of salty olives are also good for a drinking crowd. Kick up the supermarket

Spicy bites like wasabi peas and roasted pepitas will keep the drinks flowing. THE CATERING COMPANY

varieties by whipping up your own Mediterranean marinade. Get a mix of more unusual olive varieties from the olive bar, like Spanish arbequinas, French picholines, Italian Cerignolas, and oil-cured Moroccans. Slice some lemons and oranges very thinly and add to olives along with some fresh herbs, roasted red peppers, olive oil, and vinegar. You can also toast some spices, like coriander, and add to the marinade.

SUGjesTION

A Halloween Menu

- Sweet and spicy pecans
- Deviled eggs
- Butternut squash soup with roasted pepitas
- Baby back ribs with barbecue sauce
- Day of the Dead skull cookies

A Japanese Zen Menu

- Soba noodle salad
- Seaweed and daikon radish sunomono
- Negimaki (beef and scallion rolls)
- Sushi from a favorite Japanese restaurant
- Assorted dumplings with dipping sauces
- Green tea ice cream mochi for dessert

A Just-For-Guys Tailgater Menu

- Beer!
- Carmelized onion and sour cream dip with kettle chips
- Frito pie
- Hot buffalo wings with celery sticks and chunky blue cheese
- Spicy cabbage slaw
- Barbecue pulled pork on cheddar cheese biscuits
- No dessert—this menu is about salt!

Let this sit for a bit (from an hour up to two weeks). Pickles are pleasing to most as well—go for French cornichons or Italian marinated vegetables that are easy to eat and won't slop all over the place.

Crackers and prepackaged snacks from stores like Trader Joe's or Whole Foods can be a lifesaver. Beyond the chips and salsa route, you can put out bowls of Asian rice cracker mixes, wasabi peas, pretzel chips with a spicy mustard dip, pita chips with hummus, or Scandanavian crackers like caraway Finn Crisp or Ak-mak topped with cream cheese blended with dill, capers, and smoked salmon. You can also make your own crisps by toasting thinly sliced bread with olive oil, salt, and herbs.

Crudités platters are easy to compose and oh so healthy. Go beyond the baby-carrot-laden supermarket veggie sampler and use more off-the-beaten path produce, preferably what suits the season. Ransack your local farmer's market

for the best selection. You can blanch or serve raw—it's up to you. I like crudités items like sliced fennel, endive leaves, fingerling potatoes, asparagus spears, heirloom radishes, Persian cucumbers, wax beans, grape tomatoes, and jicama. Serve with nearly any dip—blue cheese works well, as does a garlic aioli. Make your own very light cheese dip by blending cottage cheese with tarragon, parsley, and diced shallot. Add some olive oil, sherry vinegar, and cracked pepper to finish. Group the vegetables by color around the plate with the bowl in the middle, and it's a beautiful sight to behold!

Cheese plates are all the rage these days, and it behooves you to experiment with more foreign flavors rather than boring cubes of Colby and pepper jack. Have at least three cheeses on the plate—a hard option (like caramel-tasting aged Gouda or a Parmigiano Reggiano), a semihard cheese (like an English cheddar or a Swiss gruyère), and a softer blue (dolce latte gorgonzola is a blue

Fry up your own tortilla chips and serve with an assortment of dips.
THE CATERING COMPANY

cheese for people who don't normally like blue cheese). Other very safe but still special cheeses are Idiazabal, Ossau-Iraty, Piave, or brebis. If people are sitting around a table, leave the cheeses whole with cheese knives so people can slice off what they want. In fact, if people are sitting down, offer them a softer, gooey cheese to try, like a triple-cream brie or a Taleggio. If people are standing up and it would be awkward to balance a plate while slicing, then slice the harder cheeses for them into wedges or matchsticks so

Offer a range of cheese options on the plate, from soft and spreadable to hard. THE CATERING COMPANY

the pork products.) If you're into smoked turkey, put out a whole smoked breast with a knife, instead of precut slices—it'll look too much like a supermarket deli platter. Another tip is to cut grilled sausage, like chicken mango sausage, on the bias, and serve it with pretzel chips and mustard sauce.

APPETIZING APPETIZERS

The next level of party food would be trays of hors d'oeuvres, either passed by servers or laid out on a buffet table for people to serve themselves. Even though hors d'oeuvres are more involved and composed, you want to try to keep them as simple as possible, or you'll go mad trying to fold two hundred and fifty dumplings all by yourself. If you don't have paid help, I strongly suggest you offer as many room-temperature or cold appetizers as possible—that way you can get them done ahead of time and manage the timing of the party better. Also, unless you're

they are easy to grab. If you're serving a softer cheese like goat cheese, roll that into truffles (balls) and cover with herbs or serve on a crostini with fig jam. People can be more concerned with how they look eating something than what they are eating, so do everything in your power to make them not look like idiots.

If you'd like to offer a meat plate, keep in mind that people are scared of visible fat, so be careful about offering the really nice Italian prosciuttos and mortadellas. Instead, try domestic prosciuttos whose fat has been trimmed or the leaner Parisian ham. Dry aged salamis are also a favorite. (It's really about hosting a party for chefs and food critics, don't go overboard with the fancy stuff. Food often intimidates people—they think certain choices are elitist and alienating. A high-end caviar bar might elicit a stampede away from your buffet table. Don't use food to show off—use it to bring people together. Make your dishes familiar, but raise the bar a little (since it is a party) by using better-quality ingredients than usual. Here are some delectable but accessible suggestions from our caterer friends:

Italian meats on a charcuterie plate is several notches above the supermarket deli platter. THE CATERING COMPANY

- Mini sandwiches: Use a cookie cutter to make bite-size rounds of white bread or brioche, then toast them. Use a demitasse spoon to add filling—anything from curried chicken salad to lobster salad—to one round and then top with another round.

- Sushi rolls from your favorite Japanese place.

- Beef, roasted, grilled or pan seared: Cut into small slivers on top of baguette slices and add a condiment of your choosing—mustard or horseradish.

- Vegetable and cheese frittata can be served at room temperature.

- Some of the big-box stores like Costco and BJs sell very good-quality frozen ethnic items, like spring rolls, pork buns, or dumplings.

- Mini burgers (called sliders) are a huge favorite. Use cocktail-size

Gazpacho soup shots are simple to serve, plus you don't need to keep it hot! THE CATERING COMPANY

potato rolls (found in grocery stores), cut a hot dog bun into thirds, or make your own little buns from premade bread dough. Make burgers ahead of time, and zap them quickly in the microwave to heat before serving.

- **Shrimp**: People go nuts for shrimp. In fact, they would probably eat their own fingers if they were dipped in cocktail sauce first.

- Soup sips served in shot glasses: Use gazpacho or another cold soup if you don't want to bother keeping the soup warm. You can use a teapot to fill people's glasses with the soup.

- Buy frozen mini tart shells (or phyllo shells) and fill them with anything! You can either heat the mixture and the shells together (as with a spinach, egg, and feta filling) or bake the shells first and fill with a room-temperature item—crab and avocado salad, herbed ricotta with caponata, blue cheese with grapes and walnuts—or a hot item, like a wild mushroom ragout (sauté mushrooms in butter and olive oil with tarragon, add Marsala wine and some stock, and let it cook down). You can put

an Asian spin on this by placing wonton wrappers in mini muffin tins and bake until hard. Fill shells with tuna tartare with seaweed salad, shrimp and mango salad, or anything vaguely Asian. You can form cups out of tortillas too—cut small rounds from corn tortillas, heat to soften, stuff into muffin tins, bake, and fill with black beans, cheese, and green chilies, or carnitas.

- Then, there's the whole subcategory of **food on sticks.** Almost anything can be skewered, cooked, and served with a dipping sauce, and the stick provides a convenient conveyance. Make sure to protect skewers from scorching on the grill.

  * Chicken satay—use thighs instead of breasts. Cover with red curry paste, ginger, and garlic, and serve a peanut sauce or a fresh mint

vinaigrette (blend rice vinegar, fresh mint, and a bit of mayo).

* Grilled lamb skewers—rub olive oil, lemon, and oregano on chunks cut from a leg of lamb. Serve with a feta cheese dipping sauce.

* Grilled vegetable skewers— good veggies to use are eggplant, zucchini, mushrooms, small onions, peppers, sweet potatoes. Serve with a roasted red pepper sauce.

* Beef skewers—most meat counters will cut kebabs for you, or you can just buy a couple of steaks, marinate them in some teriyaki sauce or a sweet soy sauce, cut them into kebabs, grill, and sprinkle with bicolor sesame seeds.

* Fish/seafood skewers—salmon, swordfish, halibut, shrimp,

scallops, and tuna all work well on a stick. Give it a Polynesian bent by adding pineapple and serving with a mango dipping sauce. Make sure to spray your grill with oil so the fish doesn't stick to the grates.

* Fruit skewers— great for luncheons or kids' parties. Stick them in a pineapple half for a Sputnik-style table display.

* Lollipop meat—lamb chops come on sticks already, which makes them the perfect party food. Have a yogurt mint dipping sauce on hand. You can make lollipops from chicken wings as well, but it takes a bit more maneuvering.

The amount of hors d'oeuvres you'll need depends a lot on the timing of your party—its duration as well as the time of day. If you're passing around trays of appetizers

for a shorter cocktail party (say, two hours), count on about six items per person for light coverage, nine to ten items per person for medium coverage, and up to fifteen per person for heavy coverage. If your party is longer than two hours and falls into the dinner hour, it's a good bet to make enough for medium to heavy eating. With hors d'oeuvres set out on platters, count on about six to nine items per guest—that should be plenty. Stagger the timing of the platters on the table too—after a couple of hours, your trays will start to look pretty crappy, so it's good to refresh the look of your buffet throughout (see **food safety** for more on this).

When composing your hors d'oeuvres trays, keep these things in mind:

• Pay attention to color. People (especially women) eat visually and are drawn to a platter with bright colors. If you're serving something neutral in tone (crostini with white bean puree,

Unless you're a professional, don't try to do a fussy architectural hors d'oeuvre. Keep it simple!
ANDRE MAIER PHOTOGRAPHY

say), try to add color by serving it on a bright plate or adding a garnish of fresh herbs or blooms. Bold color is why crudités plates are so omnipresent at parties—whether or not people love the flavor of raw vegetables, that rainbow of fresh produce looks very dramatic on a table.

- Less is always more. Don't try to do some architectural leaning tower of pizza or something because, trust me, it will not work. Keep it simple with pretty rows of food.

THE DINNER PARTY

Serving your guests a complete meal is like running the gauntlet in entertaining terms. It takes a lot of forethought and cool-headed maneuvering to get multiple courses on the table at proper temperatures at the right time. Most people don't have the oven space, let alone the fridge space, to cook and host a large-scale formal dinner party, which is why caterers have jobs. You have to pay attention to the small things, like turning up the air conditioner if the oven will be churning out heat all day long. These complications make it even more necessary for you to keep things simple. Usually when home cooks feel insecure and inexperienced in the kitchen,

they overcompensate and try to become Martha Stewart. Don't try to do some ethnic feast for fourteen people that you've never attempted before. Serve main dishes you are familiar with—roast chicken, lasagna, mac and cheese—and save the **wow-factor** foods for your appetizers or side dishes. It's also very easy to kick up an old favorite like mac and cheese with gourmet ingredients—better cheeses, a splash of truffle oil—and little changes like that can make all the difference to your guests without taking years off your life. The most important part of a menu is fresh, quality ingredients served simply; if you can get a bunch of beautiful seasonal produce from your summer farmer's market, you barely have to do anything to it for it to be a stunning success. Also remember, even the best cooks have kitchen catastrophes from time to time—that's what makes for funny stories later—so don't beat yourself up about the cold mashed potatoes or the burned roast. Learn from your mistakes, and make it even simpler the next time around.

Here are some basic dinner party menu suggestions, focusing on fast and easy. You want to shoot for a mix of premade and homemade dishes so you don't tax yourself too much on all the courses.

- Homemade pizzas, leafy salads, and slushy granitas for dessert. Buy premade pizza dough at the supermarket and jazz it up with gourmet toppings—broccoli rabe, roasted eggplant, salami like soppressata, aged cheeses, and fresh arugula tossed with lemon and olive oil. The possibilities are endless and the results are *waaaaaay* better than the delivery options.

- Chili bar! Make some vegetarian chili as the base and offer mix-ins like sautéed ground beef or turkey, roasted veggies, diced red onions, shredded pepper jack cheese, avocado, tortilla chips, sour cream, and cilantro. Serve with a simple salad, like tomatoes and corn, or oven-baked quesadillas.

- One-pot stew meals popularized in the seventies, like beef bourguignon, turkey tetrazzini, coq au vin, Swedish meatballs. With a great loaf of bread and a salad, the meal is done.

- A simple pasta—olive oil, chili flakes, grated cheese, salt, and pepper—and a salad. Or try high-quality purchased ravioli or a baked pasta like lasagne or ziti that can be premade. Pair with a couple of salads.

- Roast chicken—either home roasted or purchased rotisserie style. Serve with a salad enhanced with seasonal ingredients (berries, watermelon, and goat cheese for summer; dried cherries, blue cheese, and toasted

Roasted meats are great for a buffet spread, as they can be complemented with sauces and relishes and served at room temperature. THE CATERING COMPANY

nuts in the colder months) and good loaf of bread.

- Meatloaf with mashed potatoes and an iceberg lettuce wedge with blue cheese.

Save time by prepping your salads before the dinner party, and compose right before.
THE CATERING COMPANY

- Burgers (beef and turkey) on the grill, roasted corn on the cob, and potato salad.

Let's say you want to host a more formal, multicourse meal, like a holiday dinner. First of all, enlist help in the kitchen, whether it's a caterer, a prep person, or a cleaning person to handle the overflow of dishes. This type of meal needs to be coordinated so that each and every item is not last minute. Timing is key to getting a hot, well-prepared meal on the table, so most of the menu needs to be peppered with dishes that can be made ahead of time and simply reheated or put together before serving. Soups and salads are great for this, as are roasted vegetables. Meat roasts, like a pork loin, work well in this case as well; roasts need to sit for a while before being carved anyway, so that allows the cooking time to be completed before dinner begins. Roasts can also be served at room temperature with sweet onion relishes and different sauces and mayonnaises. Braised meats that take a while to cook, like short ribs, work great since they can be left to bubble in a slow cooker while you have a glass of champagne with your friends!

Plan a menu that fits the kitchen you have, not the kitchen you *wish* you had. For instance, no one (except Martha) has a kitchen that accommodates the myriad hot dishes needed for Thanksgiving dinner. That's why even when the turkey tastes great, all the side dishes are cold or coming out at different times. (This is when a potluck-style dinner party can really help. If you have a small oven, commit to providing the main entrée and the cold sides, and other people can bring the warm sides. Just make sure to factor in reheating time!) Most food magazines and Web sites (like epicurious.com) offer dinner party menus and timelines around major holidays. Follow these templates to give you an idea of how to orchestrate the dinner. Just, please, don't wing it.

Equally important as the timing of dishes is how well the menu fits together. Choose your main proteins first, inspired by a region you love or an option you feel comfortable with (i.e., no experiments!). Then choose your other dishes around that main dish—ask yourself, What naturally complements this entrée?

A Latin Fiesta Menu

- Margaritas, hibiscus tea, horchata
- Chips with homemade guacamole and pico de gallo
- Green chili and cheese tamales from a favorite taqueria
- Rice salad with corn, red peppers, and black beans
- Grilled beef tenderloin with a cumin dry rub, served with roasted red pepper puree or chipotle aioli
- Buy pulled pork at the deli, spice it up Mexican style, and make your own carnitas. Serve with tortillas.

Mini tortilla wraps are perfect for a fuss-free fiesta.
ANDRE MAIER PHOTOGRAPHY

A Rustic Italian Menu

- Cheese plate with a good-quality parmigiana-reggiano, sun-dried tomatoes, and olives
- Homemade crostini (olive oil and herbs, cannellini bean puree, or prosciutto and figs)
- Lasagna, classic Bolognese style or more upscale with wild mushrooms
- Tricolor salad with endive, red leaf lettuce, and arugula with vinaigrette
- Garlic bread
- Store-bought tiramisu served on flat plates with fresh berries

A Hannukah Menu

- Potato pancakes with smoked salmon, caviar, and crème fraîche

- Orange, fennel, and avocado salad

- Roast chicken

- Cider-glazed carrots

- Sufganiyot (doughnuts)

Chef Glenn Harris's Autumnal Dinner Menu

- This menu uses seasonal ingredients easily found at a farmer's market, as well as items that can be made ahead—like the tart, salad, roasted vegetables, and short ribs.

- Caramelized onions and goat cheese tart

- Butternut squash salad with arugula, pepitas, sun-dried cranberries, and apples

- Crushed Yukon Gold potatoes with bacon, sage, and sour cream

- Roasted brussels sprouts with pecans and orange zest

- Stout-braised beef short ribs

A Fancy Tea Menu

- Tea sandwiches: butter, sliced radish, and sea salt; cream cheese and cucumber, curried chicken salad with cranberries

- Mini scones with crème fraîche and preserves

- Tuna salad wraps cut into bite-size portions

- Vegetable frittatas, served cold

- Teas: iced and hot, black, green, and chai

- Assorted French macaroons for dessert—in flavors like pistachio, rose, hazelnut, and lemon

These tea pyramids with fresh herbs elevate the tea party concept.
ANDRE MAIER PHOTOGRAPHY

Starches? Condiments? Dips, sauces, slaws? Build your menu from these building blocks. Try to keep cohesion in your selections and don't mix Tuscan villa with Hawaiian luau—it'll make your guests' heads (and stomachs) spin.

Desserts and baking is a real time-consuming art, so unless you've proven yourself in this category in the past, it's best to keep to simple sweets. Nothing really beats a rich ice cream or a tart sorbet with fresh fruit in the summertime—and you can fancy it up by making a sundae in a martini glass. Layer sorbet and berries in the glass, douse with a bit of liqueur, like Chambord, and it's suddenly a beauty. The fancy-sounding granita is actually super easy—just freeze a fruit puree, mash it up with a fork, and serve in attractive glassware. Assemble a platter of gorgeous assorted cookies and chocolate truffles from a local bakery. Get old-school homey and use a Duncan Hines mix to bake a cake or some **cupcakes.** If you want

something from scratch, bundt spice cakes are simple and great for the fall, as are flourless chocolate cakes. Doctor up some store-bought items by making a brownie sundae or a homemade ice-cream sandwich. Buy an angel food cake, but whip up your own flavored whipped cream to go on top—ginger or cinnamon. If kids are invited to the party, serve root beer floats or mini milk shakes.

LET'S DO LUNCH/BRUNCH

Midday parties are fun to throw—they don't get as alcoholic and crazy as evening fetes, and you can be done with postparty cleanup by that evening. But prepping the midday meal can be just as daunting as it can be for a meal at any other time of day. Again, it's very important to prepare items that can be made ahead and served at room temperature. Everyone loves waffles and pancakes, for instance, but serving this at a party must be reserved for small gatherings since they need to be eaten fresh off the griddle. Frittatas

and quiches, on the other hand, work really well. They can be made the day before and served warmed, at room temperature, or even cold. They go well with greens or fruit and any starchy sides like a roasted sweet potato or wild rice salad. Bacon and cooked sausage are crowd pleasers and really easy to make in the oven on sheet pans for large groups.

Jewish or not, people get *meshugenah* for bagels with the works. Make up a spread with lox, nice whitefish salad from the deli, cream cheese (plain and with scallions), shaved red onion, caper berries, thinly sliced cucumbers, and tomatoes if they're in season. If the bagels are fresh, you can just warm them in the oven or serve as is. Or have a toaster on the buffet for people to toast their own—although that could cause some serious buffet clogging. To balance the savory with the sweet, put out some scones, tea breads, or pastries from a local bakery, along with some fresh seasonal fruit.

MENU

Crème brûlée–battered French toast with strawberry butter

or

Herb and sourdough frittata with savory summer tomato jam

Farm-stand melon and berry salad with lemon mint dressing

Homemade granola with orange honey yogurt

Spicy chicken breakfast sausage

Candied bacon

| CRÈME BRÛLÉE–BATTERED FRENCH TOAST |

1 loaf brioche or challah bread,
  slicked into 1½-inch slices

2 pints half-and-half

6 eggs, beaten

1 tablespoon vanilla extract

1 cup sugar

1 stick sweet cream butter,
  cut into eighths

Mix half-and-half, eggs, vanilla, and sugar. Soak bread slices in batter until wet throughout. In a large flat skillet or griddle, melt butter on medium heat and grill bread slices until golden brown.

| STRAWBERRY BUTTER |

Puree ingredients in a food processor until smooth, and chill.

1 pint strawberries

2 sticks sweet cream butter, softened
  to room temperature

2 tablespoons honey

Pinch of salt

| HERB AND SOURDOUGH FRITTATA |

Heat butter and garlic in a large sauté pan on medium heat until butter foams, then toss with bread. Season with salt and pepper, and toast in the oven on a baking sheet at 350 degrees until golden brown.

Sourdough croutons:

Small loaf of sourdough bread, crusts
  cut off and cut into ½-inch cubes

1 stick butter

1 clove garlic, chopped fine

| HERB MIXTURE |

Mix the herbs together. In a large mixing bowl combine croutons, herbs, and eggs, and season with salt and pepper. Preheat a 10-inch nonstick, ovenproof skillet or cast-iron pan in a 350 degree oven. Coat the pan with olive oil or butter, and add egg mixture without mixing in the pan. Bake in the oven about 30 minutes until set; a skewer or thin knife should come out clean.

1 bunch flat-leaf Italian parsley,
  chopped

1 tablespoon fresh oregano leaves,
  stems discarded

1 bunch chives, cut into ½-inch
  lengths

12 leaves of basil, torn

12 eggs, beaten

SAVORY SUMMER TOMATO JAM

1 yellow onion, chopped fine

2 beefsteak tomatoes (preferably
heirloom), chopped

½ cup balsamic vinegar

2 tablespoons sugar

Salt and pepper to taste

Heat all ingredients in a saucepan over medium heat until almost dry.

FARM-STAND MELON AND BERRY SALAD

1 pineapple, peeled, cored, and cut
into 1-inch cubes

1 cantaloupe, peeled and cut into
1-inch cubes

1 honeydew melon, peeled and cut
into 1-inch cubes

2 cups cubed watermelon, seeds
removed

1 pint strawberries, washed and
stemmed

1 pint blueberries, washed and
stemmed

1 pint blackberries, washed and
stemmed

Combine all fruits in a bowl. You can use or substitute whatever fruit is in season; a salad like this can't be messed up!

| LEMON MINT DRESSING |

Mix together cut fruit, and top with berries. Mix mint, lemon juice, and honey; pour over fruit and toss gently.

5 mint leaves, julienned

Juice of three lemons

2 tablespoons honey

| HOMEMADE GRANOLA |

Toast oats, sesame seeds, sunflower seeds, pecans, and coconut on a baking sheet in a 350 degree oven. Heat the butter and brown sugar in a saucepan over medium heat until sugar dissolves. Mix with the rest of the ingredients.

1 quart rolled oats

2 tablespoons sesame seeds

¼ cup sunflower seeds

¼ cup pecans

½ cup dried cherries

¼ cup shredded coconut

½ cup brown sugar

1 stick butter

| ORANGE HONEY YOGURT |

Mix together and chill. Serve with granola.

1 quart Greek yogurt

Juice of 1 orange

¼ cup honey

| SPICY CHICKEN BREAKFAST SAUSAGE |

1 pound boneless, skinless chicken thighs, coarsely ground

1 tablespoon kosher salt

1 teaspoon ground white pepper

5 leaves fresh sage, chopped

1 teaspoon ground ginger

1 teaspoon freshly grated nutmeg

¼ cup fresh parsley, chopped

2 ounces brown sugar

2 tablespoons maple syrup

1 tablespoon crushed red pepper flakes

Put chicken in a large cold mixing bowl, add all ingredients, and mix thoroughly. Form patties and grill until cooked through.

| CANDIED BACON |

1 pound lean sliced smokehouse bacon

½ pound sugar

1 teaspoon salt

1 tablespoon cracked black pepper

Preheat oven to 300 degrees. Combine sugar, salt, and pepper in mixing bowl and coat bacon well with mixture. Bake for 25 minutes on a parchment-lined baking sheet.

• ◍ •

Parties are the ideal time to eat, drink, and be merry—but don't stress too much about what kinds of sustenance you should provide at your party. As long as you provide something for your guests to nibble on and sip, whether it's potato chips and chilled beer or fancy canapés and champagne, they are going to feel taken care of. Food and drinks are comforting, and God knows everyone needs a little bit of comfort in the exciting but stressful world of socializing.

CHAPTER NINE

A Toast to the Host

Being a proper host—it's a lost art form, it seems. Even professionals like me sometimes forget the rules. I once hosted a party for some friends along with some business associates I had become close to. When the party started, I noticed a weird tension brewing in the air between these two groups; honestly, they didn't know each other very well. I realized that I hadn't done my hosting homework (i.e., before having a party, you must sit down and really think about who you are inviting and visually picture in your mind whether those people will interact well). So what should the proper host do to remedy this sort of situation? I targeted the areas at the party—like the bar and the buffet table—where I knew the two worlds would ultimately collide. I parked

If a hosting a big party like this makes you break out in a cold sweat, I can help. ANDRE MAIER PHOTOGRAPHY

myself there and began to rock out the introductions to get this melting pot boiling. And guess what? The socializing turned out to be a hit after a little bit of maneuvering on my part.

The art of being the hostess with the mostess definitely sounds retro to our modern ears, but making sure your guests are happy never goes out of style. I'll give you today's take on how to make your guests feel at ease, from timelines to table setting. I'll also cover etiquette issues like being on time, not getting drunk at your own party, and spreading yourself out among your guests.

BEFORE THE BIG DAY: MAKING TRAVEL ARRANGEMENTS FOR GUESTS

Having a destination shindig? As a host, you can do a few things to make air travel easier for your guests. Book blocks of flights for guests coming from the same place—that is, if ten guests are flying from New York, get them onto the same flight so they can carpool to and from the airport. Don't be afraid to ask for help when booking travel for multiple guests— just hire a travel agent. A capable travel specialist can help you iron out the details and find the best deals. Also, use airlines you have had a good personal experience with. You may get a great deal on Poopy Doody Airlines, but you may be setting your guests up for a horrible experience.

Destination party at the beach! Definitely help your guests find hotel rooms.
JES GORDON

Go the extra mile and have them travel in comfort. After all, their trip will set the tone for the entire event. Remember, if you book early enough you won't break the bank!

It's very gracious to do some footwork on **hotels** for your guests by scouting out the best places to stay near the location of your party. If you don't have time to check out hotels in person, it's best to stick with what you know— chain hotels. For that reason, I often gravitate toward Marriott Courtyards, Hiltons, or the trendier W Hotels. Choose a hotel that offers rooms in a range of prices. Motels are definitely cheaper than hotels: Your average Motel 6 will run from $60 to $179 per night, whereas a hotel usually starts at $179 all the way to $1,500 per night, depending on the region. Give your guests options—low-, medium-, and high-priced locations. It's important people don't feel ghetto just because they can't afford to stay at the Four Seasons—after all, this is simply a place for them to stay when they are not having fun with you. If you are planning on many people coming into town, call your choices and ask for a discounted party rate or a **room block.**

Don't flinch about asking for room discounts. Hotels make most of their money on food and beverage costs, not on their rooms. If you've ever looked at a hotel room service menu and the inflated prices, you'll know that food and drink is a free-for-all for hotels and they can charge whatever they want! Sad, but true.

MAKING ARRANGEMENTS FOR GUESTS WITH SPECIAL NEEDS

These days, it seems the peanut has become scarier than a nuclear bomb. As a host, you always need to be aware of your guests' special needs, whether it is food allergies, restrictions, or mobility issues. (If you're not sure, you can always inquire on the invitation.) Most venues must abide by wheelchair access laws, but it's always good to double- and triple-check with them beforehand if you have any disabled guests. Your house is another story, however. If there are steps at the entrance to your home, a wheelchair ramp is very easily rented for the evening. Make sure your rooms aren't cluttered with furniture or throw rugs, and always offer to bring your wheelchair-bound guests food and drinks so they don't have to make their way to the bar or buffet.

The most common food allergies involve peanuts and shellfish. If you are serving something with those elements in them, you'd be well advised to put a small tent card next to the serving platter listing the ingredients. If you're serving shellfish as a main dish, keep a nice alternative in the fridge for those who unexpectedly announce they are allergic, like a bowl of pasta and sauce that you can easily warm up at a moment's notice. Most guests with these issues will let you know beforehand (or are prepared to eat their dinner later at a burger place), but the best host will have a plan B in place. If (God forbid) a mystery allergy pops up at your dinner party, don't hesitate to call 911, and have a first-aid kit on hand. It sounds paranoid, but know the location of your nearest emergency room before you entertain.

PREPARTY NERVES

It's a rare person who can plan a party without feeling anxious. I have seen the coolest of cool, the Pinky Tuscaderos of brides, turn into absolute monsters while planning their weddings. I have seen corporate bigwigs turn into quivering bowls of Jell-O. When people have little control over an important event in their lives, it is terrifying. The smallest detail, like the thread count of a hand towel, can send them into a tailspin. But these moments can also teach you a lesson about how to keep things in perspective. Repeat after me: It's only a party. And they are just people.

I have worked with brides who are terminally ill and enjoy their wedding day and the process of planning their wedding more than any of my other clients. But it shouldn't take a terrible illness to teach us this lesson in balance and perspective. You can easily exercise this type of thinking in other ways. For example, "I can't afford to have Stevie Wonder's thirty-piece backup band for my party, but I can afford to have a smaller group of five." Bingo! If you are willing to accept certain pitfalls and spoon them onto another plate in smaller helpings, you can usually get what you want. Keep this in mind: Whether it is finding your soul mate, launching a new perfume, or making it to another birthday, you are lucky to be celebrating.

FLASH THE WARNING BEACON

As I said in chapter 2, it's a very PC thing to do to warn your neighbors that you're having a house party, and giving your immediate neighbors on either side of you a bottle of wine or some other token is a class-act thing to do. You should also give them your cell phone number so they can call if they feel the noise level is too high (hey, better you than the police.) Reassure them about the time the party is going to end, and try to stick to that number. Keep an eye on your guests as they leave to make sure they aren't too loud or trampling your neighbor's azaleas.

And always give a shout-out to your neighbors, postparty, to thank them for being so gracious.

CLEANING CREW: WHAT TO DO, WHAT TO SKIP

Being a kick-ass host is all about being proud and confident in your party environment, and taking care of your house and your belongings is a part of that process. There is a fine line between put together and having your house look *too* scoured and pristine; in the latter case, your guests won't feel like they can relax in your little wax museum. You simply want to relay to your friends that you cared enough to remove that half-eaten muffin from underneath the couch. I always have to spend about an hour stashing away all the dog toys in my home, and I find that when they are all picked up, our house looks completely transformed! For those of you with real children, you may want to do the same with the American Girl dolls and Lego sets.

Just say no to bleach products preparty—it's a real appetite killer. Choose some softly scented organic cleaners that won't overtake your space, like the Method products found at Target. A waxed wood floor looks great, but check yourself because people can slip and break their necks on the way to the snack

How to Curb Your Anxiety

- Limit your caffeine intake prior to your event. Drink your usual cup of coffee or Diet Coke in the morning but cut it out for the rest of the day to avoid insomnia, jitters, or crashing. Instead, get a decaf or herbal tea.

- Use your calendar and wireless devices to keep you on schedule. If you are a list person, then make lists—but don't create a paper volcano on your desk. Keep a pad of paper next to your bed. I guarantee that you will wake in the middle of the night with many thoughts that will disappear in the morning. Keep a pad of paper in the bathroom too— that's all I'm going to say about that.

- Visualize the type of experience you want your guests to have. Draw a "flow" map of your event: Think about where the guests will park their cars, where they will enter, where they will wander outside the main area, where they will use the restroom, where they can dance, where they can find peace and quiet, and where they will exit. If you walk through every part of your event in your mind before it occurs, you will be more aware of the twists and turns

that an event can take, and you can stay ahead of the game.

- Limit your options and go on instinct. Everybody is an expert and everybody has an opinion, so tune out the noise. Claim your event as your own, don't compare it to others, and be confident. If you throw a party with passion, it will have an infectious effect on your guests.

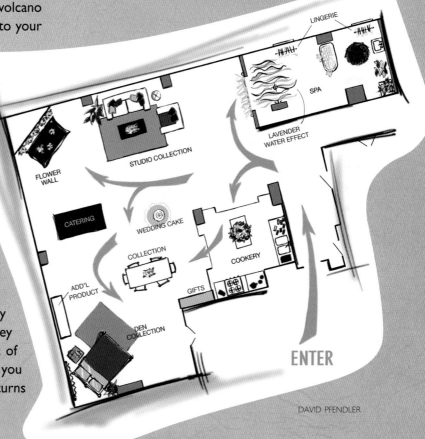

DAVID PFENDLER

These tables are perfectly set: not too cluttered and with sufficient elbow room. JES GORDON

table. If you're pressed for time, just concentrate your picking up to the party rooms, any bathrooms that may be used, and perhaps a bedroom where coats might be stored.

SETTING THE TABLE

I kind of abhor placed seating, but it can be necessary at times when you know certain people would just not mix well. If you know that your best friend from college, despite being president of a Fortune 500 company, gets absolutely whacked out of her mind on tequila and pulls her shirt off at every dinner party you've thrown, it may be best not to seat her next to the pastor from your church. I keep in mind the six degrees of separation theory when creating my seating charts; you don't want neighbors to have *too* much in common, or that will alienate them from the rest of the group, but rather there should be some interesting diversity between them. (But beware of polar opposites—that could lead to heated discussions and awkwardness for all.) Therefore, the small-business owner in an artistic field may find it wonderful to sit next to a knowledgeable accountant, which may lead to a wonderful conversation about structuring a

creative business. Just put yourself in your guests' shoes and ask yourself, What would I want in this situation? A lot of hosts will insist on splitting up couples at a dinner party, but I think that's unnecessary. I personally hate it when Bill and I haven't seen each other all week because of work and we go to a dinner party and are told we can't sit near each other. Most happy, healthy couples will be able to handle sitting next to each other and engaging those around them. If ultimately you're at a loss on where to place your guests, just give it up and let the chips fall where they may. And after a while people will shift around a little to make themselves more comfortable. You don't really want to nail people down to their seats anyway, so giving them the opportunity to get up and dance or take coffee and dessert in another area is usually a welcome change. That way, they can chat up people who may have caught their attention during dinner. I once designed a dinner party for young single types with a speed-dating sort of table arrangement where they changed seats after every course. And it was actually fun—and, I think, successful on the romantic front!

Now, onto the actual table setting. Here are several rules that will not only ensure a beautiful table but a functional one as well.

1. Ideally, each person should be given enough room when seated at the dining table. That means your chairs should be able to house a two-foot-wide tushy and your place settings should be at least a hand's width apart. Allow for extra space on the table if you are using a decorative charger plate; an average dining plate is ten inches in diameter, and a charger plate usually starts at thirteen inches.

2. Again, your centerpiece should not exceed the height of your fingertips when placing your

This table is packed with place settings, but doesn't feel overly cluttered with utensils or glassware. JES GORDON

elbow on the table and pointing your hand straight up toward the ceiling.

3. Even if you are serving many types of beverages, keep the number to three glasses per person. Too much glassware on the table is often a recipe for disaster.

4. Make all utensils easily accessible. The small salad fork goes on the outside and to the left of your larger main course fork. Your knife is to the right of your dinner plate and often a soup spoon is placed on the outside right of the knife. If you are serving a specialty like steak that requires another kind

of knife or if you need a small dessert spoon, I like to place that over the top of the plate horizontally, otherwise the sides get way too cluttered. Offer your guests new silverware between courses—making them eat their tiramisu with a used soup spoon is not cool. If you have to, buy some cheap sets of silverware for your party at IKEA, Target, or even a dollar store.

5. Don't clutter the tabletop with too many candles in the reach line—if guests reach for the butter dish, they shouldn't have their hand incinerated. Try to visualize how people will reach for dishes throughout the evening, and try to create a path for them to do so. Also, don't place candles too close to a floral centerpiece. Burned flowers ain't pretty. Put your candles in glass hurricanes or holders. Long and lean tapers are very elegant, but they can also be quite drippy and messy. If candles aren't cutting the mustard, keep LED votives in mind as an option.

6. Make sure your chairs are stable and comfortable enough to encourage people to stay seated.

7. Level your table if your floor is uneven—simply shove a matchbook or folded paper under the shorter leg to keep the jiggles (and spills) at bay.

STOCKING THE BATHROOM WITH GOODIES

Here's a confession: I adore perusing bathrooms and testing out every toiletry I can get my hands on. I thrill when I attend an event and there are lovely little soaps and hair ties to try out. Thus, I am a firm believer in providing **amenities** at every party, if you can muster it. I am not a woven basket type of girl, so I like to display guest toiletries on a cool serving tray on a small table in the bathroom. There are some fun little tables that are specifically made to fit right into the corner of a room, and these are perfect for bathrooms. If you can't fit an occasional table in the room, it's OK to keep the essentials (hand soap and lotion) on your sink and set up a mini vanity area right outside the bathroom—as long as it's not in the middle of the party! Hang a full-length wall mirror behind a little table with your primping accessories.

WHAT TO WEAR, DARLING

When I am putting together an event, I bring a big gym bag with all my "in case" items: extra socks, sole pads for sore feet, and three changes of clothing—one for the initial setup, one for the event, and one for the breakdown. This is obviously geared toward professional schleppers, but thinking in terms of pregame/game/postgame is useful even for the home host. Pregame, your clothes and shoes should be comfortable; look for shoes that let your feet expand, since you'll be stuffing your toes into more formal shoes at the event itself. At the party, I think high heels are just silly if you're the host and need to run around—but if you *really* need that height, go for a rubber-bottomed wedge heel, which softens the blow of hardwood floors. This is the most important thing—with confidence comes style. Wear whatever makes you feel like a rock star, and wear what is comfortable. One of my good event planner friend's signature look is complementing her all-black outfit with an Alexander McQueen skull-and-crossbones-patterned scarf; it makes her feel like she is still exuding her personal style while working an event. I have another buddy who always wears peacock feather earrings when she is hosting events . . . we call her Miss Peacock.

Now for makeup and hair. It's not like you're the queen of Mardi Gras, so coiffing your hair into a beehive or painting your face within an inch of its life is just too weird. For makeup, shoot for durable brands (waterproof mascara, long-wearing lipstick) that you won't have to worry about reapplying during the party. Better yet, stay away from the dramatic pigments—I usually just keep a stick of Burt's Bees or Blistex Silk & Shine in my pocket to keep my lips glossy. Overall, it's most important to present yourself as you normally do so your guests feel at home and recognize you as the person they know as their friend.

As an event planner, my favorite accessories aren't hoop earrings or a fierce snakeskin belt—it's a small black backpack filled with geeky necessities that I need within arm's reach. I think every host should also have a stash of emergency gear. If you have poor eyesight, make sure to bring along extra contact lenses, saline solution, or an extra pair of glasses. Always have something on hand to freshen your breath even if you have to steal mints from the bathroom. As a host, stay hydrated and make sure you smell nice and clean from your armpits to your mouth. If your event is outdoors, pack some sunglasses, sunscreen, a sun hat, and bug repellant. As far as jewelry is concerned, play it simple and elegant. Wear pieces that aren't cumbersome or that will dangle into the punch bowl. If your jewelry box is bare, look into borrowing for the night. I've seen hosts approach a favorite family jeweler to lend them something fabulous to wear at their event. If your vendor decides to be generous with you, be sure to insure what you are borrowing. Take out a temporary certificate of insurance on your goods until they are returned safely (call your regular insurance provider for details).WARNING: You may suffer mild depression when forced to give these items back.

If you're hosting at a venue, bring a bag full of tricks to get you through the night. DAVID PFENDLER

You can't do it alone, people. If you don't have an army of interns to assist you, feel free to enlist your nearest and dearest. My husband, Bill, is often my wingman at events. If he isn't working at his *real* job, I grab his ass and force him to work for me. At our own parties, we take turns talking to guests and making sure the food table and bar are stocked; we meet up with each other every half hour or so to talk strategy on music, food, and the guests. Even if we don't see much of one another at the party, it's great to recap with each other when it's over.

I also like to enlist my friends for my events—they are a grab bag of talents that I can exploit for my own purposes! I have silk screener friends who can provide one-of-a-kind T-shirts for my kids' parties, I have DJ friends who constantly keep me hip, and I have chef friends from whom I pilfer cocktail and food concoctions. But don't enlist friends

Will you have a waitstaff at your event? Sometimes it's fun to provide cool accessories for them too. If your party has a gold color scheme, give your male staff gold ties. Your waitstaff should be equipped with extra lighters and pens, but please ask them to remove any business cards from their pockets; it's poor taste for vendors to advertise at an event. Good things come to those who wait—let the impressed guests call the host and ask for referrals!

who are invited to a party. Events are hard work, and your friends should be allowed to enjoy themselves and not stress out over the vodka supply that is running low or a clogged toilet. This can end up in some resentful feelings in the long run.

The biggest suckers to help you throw a party are family members, because you know that even though they may hate you for a few hours, you are in fact family and they have no choice but to love you in the end. My mother happens to be an awesome florist and I call her in often to help us with a massive production for parties. She and my brother are also musicians, so I can often go to them for music advice.

If you have decided to cook for your own dinner party, it's worth the investment to hire someone to help you keep the kitchen organized and the dishes cleaned and ready to go for the next course. It's inappropriate to sit among your guests in a dirty apron and rubber gloves, so treat yourself to someone who can keep things churning behind the scenes.

THE PARTY TIMELINE

The timing of an event is *everything*. I just planned a wedding, and much to my dismay, the couple insisted that it be very casual and not follow a timeline. I knew that this was a recipe for disaster, but they insisted (rudely), and I decided to let them have what they wanted. So the evening goes on and things are going pretty well until I look at the clock and I realize that the party had fifteen minutes to go and the wedding cake hadn't been brought out. The cake appeared just as the lights were coming on for the venue staff to break the room down—it sucked, and the night ended on a sour note.

Timelines for large events can be very involved and down to the last millisecond when dealing with everything from shuttle bus schedules to vendor load-in and setup to **toasts** and band breaks. These timelines should be created by a party professional. But for the smaller, hands-on party, there are some simple rules to follow.

COUNTDOWN TO THE PARTY

- The day before the party, I clean the shit out of my house. Then I don't let anyone, including my husband and three pets, move until after the party.

- During cleanup time, put away any embarrassing or valuable items and store them in a closet your guests won't have access to.

- Map out places where guests can store coats or baggage in your house, whether it is an extra bedroom or a spacious hall closet. Stock the area with hangers.

- Several hours before the event, start chilling your wine or champagne along with prepping any food you are serving.

Get your candles lit in advance of your guests' arrival so you don't have to worry about it. ANDRE MAIER PHOTOGRAPHY

- About three hours before, do an honest evaluation of how your house smells. Have some incense or sage on hand to give the place an odor overhaul and allow the house to absorb the smell in plenty of time before the party begins. You don't want your place reeking of Glade.

- Be party ready at least an hour before the event begins. You should be showered and dressed, all trash and setup debris should be gone, and all coasters, trash cans, toilet paper, hand towels, food stations (serving platters), and bar elements (glassware and liquor) should be in place and ready for use.

- Chop up lemons, limes, or other drink garnishes you need for the bar and place them in the fridge.

- Put all candles where they belong and have the wick facing up so you can light them easily. You can light candles forty-five minutes before call time (make sure the candles have at least a ten-hour life span).

- If you are serving hummus and pita or veggies and dip, put all your premade stuff into attractive bowls (instead of leaving them in the containers they came in) and store in your fridge. Don't put snacks out too early to avoid the yucky crust that forms on top of food. This will also prevent you from eating it all before your guests arrive.

- Keep backup food close by to refurbish the snacks. Use chip clips for freshness, and cover food properly and refrigerate.

- Put the ice for drinks in a watertight bucket a half hour before guests arrive. Don't worry—unless your home is an oven, ice takes longer to melt in large quantities than you think.

- Serving some frozen appetizers? Get them all onto pans and start preheating that oven in time for the first batch of snacks to be ready at least twenty minutes before game time. People always show up early, so make sure they can get a drink and a snack while they sit there feeling embarrassed because they are the first ones to show.

- Don't put on your high heels until the very last minute. Keep them close in case you have some early birds, but let those feet hang out before they go to prison for the night.

Now down to the nuts and bolts of timing. When I have guests coming for a sit-down meal, I always like to start with an official cocktail hour with drinks and small bites of food like cheese, fruit, and nuts, just to tempt their palates. Cocktail hours are for socializing and getting that first warm splash alcohol into your system (or for some, that jolt of caffeine). If your party includes a little dancing, sometimes I'll crank up the volume on the tunes a little, right when the cocktail hour is ending, so the guests can fit in a quick dance set before having to settle down and behave for dinner. Keep an eye on timing—you don't want your party to turn into a slumber party, so keep each element short and sweet. Predinner dancing should be fifteen minutes long, tops. It's good to fit dancing in between important layers of the evening. You don't want people getting down during dinner, but it works to turn up the music in between dinner and dessert, just to break things up and give you time to clear the table.

Toasts should be made very early in the evening because the people giving them tend to fret. Letting them get it over with is the nicest thing you can do. Plus, late-night toasts are invariably drunken speeches that drone on and on—not fun. I encourage toasts right when people are sitting down to dinner. Cocktail hour is for networking and it's not cool to harsh on that vibe, but when people first get settled at the table, they are more alert and receptive. Simply clink your glass with silverware to signify that a toast is coming up and to shush everyone, and segue into introducing the toaster to the party. When asking a friend or family member to give a toast, give them a three- to five-minute maximum, no longer than the wait at your average traffic light.

If you want to move the party from one area to another, remember that guests are like cattle and they need to be prodded. I would use a cattle prod if I was legally allowed to, but since I can't, I usually circulate around the room, tapping shoulders and telling people politely to move on to the dinner area. If you have support staff, divide up this task so it doesn't take all night. Sometimes people will blatantly ignore your request—don't get pissed, but keep up the gentle reminders. Guests need to be given time to relocate—to finish up a conversation, finish a drink, or use the restroom—so allow at least ten to twenty minutes of herding time.

Preparations for coffee and dessert should begin when your guests are halfway through their meal. This allows for a more seamless transition between courses.

The wine has been sipped, the truffles nibbled, the room trashed. Now how do you signal to your guests that it's time to leave without turning on the overhead lights? The first way is to simply let them know on the invitation what the time of the party is, à la 7:00 p.m. to midnight. Most of the time, guests at a dinner party will know by intuition that when the last piece of piecrust has

been eaten or when the sambuca bottle is put away, it's their cue to split—but that delineation can be more difficult with a raging disco party with endless tequila shots. In that case, you may be forced to travel around the room, thanking people for coming, and they will most likely get the hint. If they don't, then simmer down the music, clear away the food, and close up access to the alcohol. Once people think alcohol is going away, they will too. If you have some dingleberry stragglers after all this work, there is nothing wrong with being honest and stating: "Guys, it's been an awesome evening but I am wrecked! Thank you so very much for coming and we will do it again soon, but get out of my house." And then smile . . . really big.

GUEST MANAGEMENT: HANDLING HOST GIFTS

Since I am not two years old, I don't open or display any gifts that my guests bring me at an event. It's

not like there is a present table at a dinner or cocktail party; if someone gives me a great bottle of booze, and my bar area is already set up, I'll enjoy the gift at a later date (by myself!)—unless the guest obviously wants me to open up this particular bottle at this party. I usually bring gifts to another room, like an extra bedroom or the kitchen if there is space available. If someone brings you an ugly bouquet of flowers, you have to suck it up and put those puppies in some water—it's not the flowers' fault, but you also don't need to make it your centerpiece. Gifts are gestures of appreciation and should be gracefully accepted, but they don't need to be the focal point of your party.

OFFERING DRINKS

I don't love it when people offer drinks at the door—people get drunk too fast and the evening ends a lot earlier than expected. I like for people to come inside, get acclimated, put down their coats, and make their way over to the bar area in their own time. Nonetheless, if you're hosting a large affair in a venue and your guests are being held in a waiting area before going into a ceremony or presentation, it's very nice to give them something to wet their whistle—like sparkling water or lemonade in the summertime or hot apple cider in the winter. Otherwise, I feel that people should wait until they settle into the event before they are offered any drinks.

MASTERING THE MINGLE

Be a voyeur who can listen to several conversations at once, and jump on any chance you can to connect your guests. Make sure your introductions have meat. Don't just say, "This is so-and-so," and walk away. Say, "This is Bob. He works in advertising and just launched a doggy fashion line with his partner, and they just came back from a fabulous tour of the flea markets in the South of France!" Try to introduce people whose interests coincide as well. Usually you need to physically bring people to one another, or station yourself at a gathering place, such as the bar or buffet, where people are waiting around. It's smart to do your homework and find out what's going on in your guests' lives, and then use that info to play connect the dots. If people still stand around awkwardly after your meaty intro, then recognize you can only do so much for the socially backward.

The best way to promote mingling is to provide the aforementioned gathering spots, like a buffet table or bar area—even a line to get into the restroom! Create standing gathering areas and other lounge/seating areas. Guests who choose to sit in a group of furniture all facing each other will generally not be able to avoid introducing themselves! Playing games is another great way to break the ice between guests. At one of our cocktail parties guests met each other while waiting in line for their turn at the Dance Dance Revolution game we had set up in our backyard.

The key to successful hosting is to spread yourself out among your guests. I like to call myself the Stealth Cricket. At parties, I hop around continuously and land for about ten minutes maximum in an area and then hop again to my next mingling spot. It's important not to let any guest monopolize your time at an event, and your excuse is simply: "Gotta go, I am running the party." You need to check on the oven or take Aunt Frieda's coat or replenish the toilet paper. Keep moving as if you have a hula-hoop on your hips that could drop to the ground if you stood still.

WHEN TROUBLE COMES KNOCKING

As a good host, it's equally important not only to know how to do things right, but to know what to do when things go wrong. This is where ad-libbing comes into play.

When the going gets tough, one simply must make shit up.

A calm ad-libber is a successful ad-libber. If situations go awry, keep your cool. If your toilet clogs up or a candle flame decides to travel outside its designated area, stop for a moment and let yourself think. It may sound paranoid, but always have a plan B. For example, if you hire a band or DJ for your event, always have another one in your back pocket that you would feel comfortable calling up in case the original choice doesn't come through. Educate yourself on the surroundings: Know where all the emergency exits are in any place you decide to use and make sure they are very visible to your guests. Make sure you have fire extinguishers readily available in several areas of your venue, including your home. Be sure to have plenty of extra paper products on hand such as toilet paper, paper towels, and extra napkins. You should also make sure that your bathrooms are equipped with plungers, extra garbage can liners, a first-aid kit, and room spray! Case the room every half hour or so—take a stroll through your event to take an inventory of what is happening and if there are any activities that you need to pay special attention to. Check all the bathrooms, kitchen area, and of course the main guest locations to ensure that everything is still running smoothly and to be able to stop any disasters that may occur. Hosting is a very exhausting job; you need to stay as sober as possible so you can hop into action if needed.

THE LATECOMERS

Your guests will all arrive at different times, late and early. It's slightly annoying when guests arrive early, but not as annoying as late guests (especially at a dinner party). Nonetheless, the train must leave the station, and late guests will just have to jump on as best they can or simply decide not to come. If guests arrive late, you do not have to be responsible for helping them catch up. However, certain situations are beyond people's control; hopefully, they would call you and tell you they are running very late because of a traffic jam or some other circumstance, but if they simply decide to saunter in as the main course is wrapping up, that is their problem. I suggest you just move on as scheduled—no offers of the predinner and dinner fare. As a host, you need to focus on keeping a good, consistent flow in the room and not stop the vibe because someone is being disrespectful. I would hope that this person would know enough to slip into the room quietly and try to meld in smoothly. A guest showed up very late at one of my parties and felt guilty about it, so instead of slipping in quietly, she clearly felt as if she needed to make a big announcement that she had finally arrived! The entire room just stopped, looked at her, and then went back to what they were doing. It was disruptive—and more embarrassing for the guest in the long run.

LAYING OFF THE SAUCE

I can't tell you how many times I have watched brides starve themselves and then go ape shit on booze and food at their wedding, only to end up saying "I do" to a toilet. It's also unnerving to go to a cocktail party and see your host retire to her bedroom forty minutes into the celebration. Of all people present, the host should be alert to everything at the event. That's why I typically nurse one glass of wine for the duration of my parties. Unfortunately, you are responsible for your guests and if they need anything (or even require medical attention), you have to be on your game to give it to them. Needless to say, the same goes for illegal drugs at your party—you are the one responsible. If you feel left out of the action, do some end-of-the-evening shots with your friends. But you don't just need to worry about your own blood-alcohol level—as a host, you also need to cut off guests who are getting too inebriated. Kindly tell them that you cannot serve them alcohol anymore, and that you are doing this for their own good. Arrange for a taxi or car service to take them home, if needed (see **transportation for the tipsy**). If they get belligerent, well, then on to the next topic.

HOW TO DEAL WITH UNRULY JACKASSES

Find the largest guy at your party and have him throw their ass out. If that seems a little harsh, here are some kinder, friendlier options for the out-of-control partygoer.

1. If you know that certain friends have the propensity to get drunk and disorderly, talk to them before the party and ask them to keep it under control. Gently tell them that you'll be forced to kick them out if they break this understanding.

2. At the party, pull them aside and see if you can speak reasonably to them about simmering down.

3. Appeal to their sense of guilt, like a Jewish mother. Make it a point to say, "You're ruining this party."

4. Ask for support from the person who accompanied them.

5. Don't feel guilty for throwing someone out if you feel they're endangering people at your event—or even just the good time that is meant to be had. Feel free to call local authorities if you need to. Anyone who would act this way at your party isn't a good friend anyway.

THE INEVITABLE SPILLAGE

If a spill occurs at your party, treat it like a time bomb and deal with it immediately instead of waiting until the party is over—otherwise it'll just get harder to clean. If someone spills something, they will not be embarrassed that you cleaned it up right away. No doubt, they'll be relieved when they see they didn't ruin your furniture!

I am a big believer in natural removers like soda water and salt for nearly all party stains—wine, food, gravy, and, yes, vomit. Don't rub a cloth into the stain, as that will just grind the nastiness further into your fabric. Just pour a large amount of soda water onto the stain to create a fluid surface, and blot with a paper towel or white cloth towel to suck up the stain. Or use a great commercial cleanser like OxiClean and water to saturate the spill before blotting. For stains like red wine, use a thick covering of kosher salt over water to absorb the spill instead of paper towels.

• • •

Being a good host is a valuable skill set to master because it involves major multitasking and keeping cool under pressure. Once you've mastered parties, you can master anything! Having said that, here's the most important part: Parties are supposed to be fun, and hosting parties should be fun as well. Being a host means you've got friends and family to celebrate with, and that's a good thing. So think positively, and try not to get bogged down in all the details. A good host is not a diva or a stress monster. She's out there in the party, knocking back a drink and having a blast.

A sprinkle of salt and some soda water will take care of the nastiest spills, I swear!
DAVID PFENDLER

CHAPTER TEN

After the Party's Over

The end of the party can be met with a mixed bag of emotions, ranging from "How can I get these drunk idiots out of my house?" to "I feel like a rock star! I've never seen people having so much fun!" The latter is what I hope you feel after throwing your party—but this has less to do with the success of the party and more to do with your mind-set. If you reconcile yourself to the notion that things are going to go wrong (though your guests would probably never guess it), and that short of a flash flood, anything is fixable, then you'll probably exit the party feeling pretty good. Make a pact with yourself that this will be an enjoyable experience, not a drain on your nerves or a thankless chore. If you keep this perspective and go into the event thinking things

will be great, I can assure you that postevent, you'll feel the same way.

As the party winds down, you should too. You made it! Ignore the dish pile in the kitchen or the peanuts that rolled their way into the floor vents, and spend a few last moments with your guests. This is a really great time to express to your friends how happy you are that they came and to simply connect with people. It's ironic because throwing an event can seem like all work and no play—maybe that's why some of my most memorable moments are when I'm saying good-bye to people. It's the first chance I've had to really talk to my friends all night!

But just because the energy is winding down doesn't mean you don't have things to consider as a host. Here are the final things you

need to think about before calling it a night.

YOU'RE NEVER TOO OLD FOR PARTY FAVORS

At an event I set up, we wrote guest names for seating assignments on little rocks in gold metallic ink. For some reason, the guests at this party became obsessed with those rocks. They were fiddling with them all night, and at the end of the evening we had all of these drunken adults coming to us practically in tears because they had lost their rock. What this story tells me is that people love simple and nostalgic things. Not long ago we held a "pure fun" party given by a family who just wanted to get together with their favorite friends and family members. For favors, we gave out

Rubik's Cubes, jacks sets, Silly String, and Slinkys, and the kids and adults went nuts.

To me, the best parting gifts are leftovers, like flowers, or extra brownies wrapped up in tin foil. You can get fancy and buy those Chinese take-out boxes from pearlriver.com so your guests can take home leftovers in fun packages. I particularly love getting some sort of doughnut, cookies, or my favorite M&M's on the way out of a party. I have usually been drinking and dancing all evening and I'm craving something sweet to keep my energy up. I've seen hosts hand out cups of French fries, or hire a Krispy Kreme doughnut truck waiting outside the party. For my wedding I did something fabulously hokey—we gave out M&M's with my dogs' faces on them, which we designed right on the M&M's Web page. If you buy candy in bulk, you can save a dime or two (one of my favorite sites is economycandy.com). You can wrap the candy in small cellophane bags that you can order from uline.com.

For flowers, I like to create little cash-and-carry bouquets from my centerpiece flowers by having some of those cellophane flower sleeves on hand. They make it easy to create a little bouquet bundle for your guests. By giving away real elements from the party, you are keeping the memory of the celebration fresh in your guests' minds and not distracting them with something cute but unconnected like a miniature bonsai tree when your party had nothing to do with Asian themes or botanicals.

But really, don't feel pressured to give a parting gift at your party. I have often found that people are sometimes annoyed by having to take things home where it will join legions of clutter and junk and ultimately end up in the garbage. If you want to thank your guests for coming, then just say that to them; if you feel desperate to hand out a trinket of thanks, then give something that reflects the concept of your party. If you had a room full of candles at your party, stay consistent and give away a candle as a parting gift. Guests will think of you and your party the next time they light that candle in their own home. If your event is for charity, then guests should receive some sort of note thanking them for their donation. Or if it's a social event, you can make a donation to a specific charity in their name. For the parting gift, give guests a simple card explaining the charity and why it's important to you. I like planting trees at Trees for the Future (trees ftf.org), which sends the donor a certificate saying where the tree was planted.

You don't want the parting gift to take over the party itself, so if you can't get to it or can't deal with it, then just focus on the party and make that as good as it can be. I don't think there will be many complaints about why there isn't

These orchids from the table centerpiece would make lovely "to go" gifts for guests. ANDRE MAIER PHOTOGRAPHY

some tacky T-shirt awaiting your guests upon their departure.

WHEN YOU JUST CAN'T SAY GOOD-BYE . . .

Despite all logic and reason, after parties have become an important part of many events I produce. (In fact, grooms seem more likely to plan the after party than the wedding itself.) Why are they so popular? Many hosts just want to misbehave once an event is finally over—everyone gets to get sloshed without offending Nana or the boss. Frequently, hosts don't have time to chill with their friends during their parties because they are busy with introductions, shilling hors d'oeuvres, and giving thank-you speeches. Thus, the party givers need to give *another* party so they can actually have a good time. The initial excitement of the after party gets everyone through the first round of drinks, but by the second or third round, people start losing it. It's all slurry speech, smeared lipstick, and gratuitous "I love yous" from that point on. It's a shame when the debauchery of after parties erases the elegance of the event itself, so all I ask is that you take on this task with a solid dose of moderation. Instead of drinking enough alcohol to quench the thirst of Russia, switch to water or Gatorade so you'll be able to remember the night with fondness (or just remember the night, period). If you are serving alcohol, offer the same selection as before so your guests don't mix it up too much. And make sure there is plenty of bottled water on hand.

PUTTING YOUR HOUSE BACK TOGETHER AGAIN

I say, clean up after an event like your life depended on it! The

After-Party Ideas

- A slick club with a cash bar. You've already hosted an event earlier that evening—let your guests buy you a drink now!

- A dive bar. Complete the look with hard-rock jukebox, pool table, and darts.

- A karaoke bar. At this point, people are fully loaded and ready to make complete asses of themselves. You might as well take advantage of this.

- A Japanese teahouse. Soothing and classy with bubble tea and mochi ice-cream treats.

- A local diner. There's nothing better for soaking up alcohol than greasy omelets and short stacks!

thought of a five-month-old cheese chunk residing under your couch is horrifying. Hire a cleaning crew if you need to. Throw away your garbage responsibly, and recycle what you can. Toss the empty bottles in a recycling bin; if you have to drive to one, make sure you give them a quick rinse so your car doesn't end up smelling like skunky old beer. If you have created an enormous amount of garbage (or expect to do so), you can call to warn your local garbage service. You can even order a small Dumpster to be brought to your house that will be collected later.

When you have a bunch of food leftovers for a large event, I suggest calling a local homeless organization and asking them if they take donations. Some agencies are not able to take cooked dishes because of liability issues, but if you have fresh produce or unopened canned or boxed goods that you don't think you will use in the future, then give it away. Local hospitals and old folks homes may want your leftover flowers, but I have found more than once that they don't have the ability to come and retrieve them; if you really want to give something back to your community, then be prepared to drop these items off yourself. Wrap up the leftover lasagna and offer it to any staff who helped you. I assure you, they will be hungry as hell after watching you and your friends gorge yourselves all night! A friend of mine started an awesome Web site called usedeventstuff.com, which allows you to post your used event items (hard goods) on his site where it can be sold to other folks around the country. We have often given an enormous amount of our event props to an organization called Materials for the Arts. For us, it's a real coup when we get letters from art/theater majors or community theaters expressing their thanks for some random bolt of gold organza fabric we gifted to the organization.

THE ART OF THE THANK-YOU NOTE

If guests bring gifts to your party, act as if you were raised right and send them a big ol' thank-you postparty. As guests arrive, keep some small Post-its close by to tag the gift with the name of the gifter in case people don't include cards and just hand you bottles of wine (although take note—this is why it's important to always include a card with your gifts!).

These days it's really a piece of cake to say thank you with the world of e-cards, e-mails, and cell phones, so not saying thanks is pretty inexcusable. When I get the urge to actually put pen to paper, I like to buy cute thank-you cards, which are everywhere these days! When I am not in the mood to chicken-scratch a handwritten note, it's completely cool with my friends to send a heartfelt e-mail expressing my genuine thanks. I have even texted my thank-yous! The point is to say it—it doesn't really matter how.

Another way to say thank you is to throw another party. If we find that we have a large amount of alcohol or food left over, sometimes I will ask folks to come over for a more relaxed gathering, maybe on a Sunday when the boys are watching sports. I get to have more one-on-one conversations at this type of get-together, so that's fun.

POSTPARTY DEPRESSION

This is one of the saddest scenarios I see in my business. I deal with people who are sometimes planning an event for years—they put their entire lives into it, sometimes forgetting about their jobs and personal life just to plan the perfect party. Sometimes the adrenaline and excitement of throwing a party is something that people get addicted to, much like drugs or chocolate. So when the party is over, they are left with that empty-nest feeling and nothing to look forward to. And that's why planning a party should be a

Cheer up, lady! Just because the party is over doesn't mean your life is over.
DAVID PFENDLER

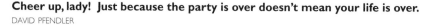

part of your life but not the whole thing.

It's not as if this were the only party you'll throw. I usually have one party at my house per year, so when one ends, I'm already thinking and excited about the next one. It's hard to think this

way when weddings are concerned because (hopefully) you won't be throwing one every year, but you can renew your vows or celebrate your marriage through anniversaries for many years to come. There is always a reason to party! You got an A on your term paper, you lost five pounds, you got promoted, you got fired, you got married, you got divorced, your kid finally got potty trained . . . whatever!

Here are a few mental tricks to keep postparty depression at bay:

- Don't let everything else in your life go to hell while you're planning this thing. Keep a balance between work, your love life, kids, nutrition, emotional well-being, and your party; it's just one part of the Chex mix.

- Don't let the party define you—you define it. This way you don't feel as if you don't know who you are outside of being a party girl. So dress like yourself (with an added touch of flair maybe) but keep your everyday feet on the ground and don't get completely lost in the fantasy, because reality is waiting just around the corner.

- Don't forget who your friends and family are during the planning process. Though you may be stressed out, don't abuse those around you. You'll need them later.

- Don't overextend your budget to the point that you resent ever having a party in the first place. If you don't stick to some monetary restrictions, the party itself can become your nemesis.

LEARNING FROM YOUR MISTAKES

My smart father once said to me, "Jes, it's OK to make mistakes. Just try not to make them more than twice." We are all human and we screw up from time to time, so cut yourself some slack. Here are some of the most common party mistakes that people make—but hopefully not more than twice!

- Bad music: Know your crowd and choose your playlists

accordingly and play them at a bearable volume. If you are having a ladies' tea, Guns N' Roses is a poor choice.

- Overcrowded space: In this situation people feel as if they are in a coffin all night, which is not a pleasant feeling. Make sure your party space can accommodate the number of people on your guest list.

- Hot air: If I go to a party and it's hotter than a crotch, I am out of there! A colder-than-average room is more tolerable since it will heat up with bodies in there, but a stuffy room will only get worse.

- Too outdated: A lot of people are stuck in the past and think they know what a good party looks like—too bad their ideas are from 1952. Keep your eyes open to the choices available nowadays. Instead of your famous ambrosia salad, this time rock out a more progressive edamame salad!

- Running out of libations: I am semicool with running out of alcohol, because if you bought plenty and your guests went through it, they *should* switch to water at that point. But if it's a case of bad math, then that's a party killer. Figure out how much alcohol you need and buy a little more than that, since there's nothing wrong with having a little leftover alcohol in the house. Keep your ice supply stocked too!

- Power outages: There's nothing worse than a blackout at a party. If you are having a house party, make sure you have plenty of candles and flashlights on hand, just in case. If you happen to have a backup generator lying around, that's great too. If you are having a party professionally produced, be sure the power

suppliers bring plenty of backup.

AND DID YOUR PARTY EXPRESS YOU?

I would suppose that people come to your parties because (a) they like you enough to be there, and (b) they can't wait to be part of your world in a celebratory way. My friends know that if I'm going to throw a party, it is going to rock! It's not because of the money I spend or the food or even the alcohol—it's because nothing makes me happier than watching my friends and family feel happy. I always make that possible by playing their favorite tunes, serving their favorite foods, lighting the place so they don't look old, and simply catering to their good time ahead of my own.

Everything I have spoken about in each chapter of this book should reflect you as the host. If you are being suffocated by overbearing forces (like a mother-in-law or whomever), stick to

your guns. Your guests have to recognize you in the event. Even if it's something small, like naming the **specialty drink** or choosing the color of the flowers or even the hand towels in the bathroom, you have to express yourself. I'm obviously a seasoned party thrower and I've heard through the grapevine that people say, "We want to go to a Jes Gordon party, no doubt!"—which means that something I did at my parties made them mine. And it made people want to come back again.

This takes confidence and knowing who you are, which is easier said than done. If you are not confident in your party style, then God bless Martha Stewart—that's why she sells a lot of magazines. I think with a few logistical production tips, we humans should be able to find our event style within ourselves, even if we have to wear earplugs while listening to our mother-in-law's opinions.

Here are some of my tips on uncovering your personal party style:

- Take a look in your closet. If most of your clothes are funky and contemporary, go a little looser and more modern at your party. If everything is Burberry and buttoned up, then old-school formal is more your thing.

- Try to visualize every element of your party in your head before it happens. Are you happy with the way things are going? If not, make changes before the party even begins.

- Play some tunes at home and see if your hips start swaying.

- If you can, taste the wine or food you are serving before your event so you can see if the flavors suit you. If you are serving a specialty cocktail you have concocted on your own, *definitely* taste it before serving it at your party.

- Don't become someone else and create a fake party persona. Be yourself, with more energy.

• ● •

The fact is, people usually make mountains out of molehills when it comes to parties. Stop looking at a party like it's a rare animal you've never seen before. We've all been partying since our first birthdays! So take a breath, stand back, and realize that people are pretty easy to please. I find that when your guests get a chance to call a babysitter and go out, just that is sometimes enough to make them happy. People like to eat, talk, drink, poop, dance, watch TV, make money, laugh, and have sex—it ain't rocket science. If you can cover just a couple of those things at your party, you are going to have a great night.

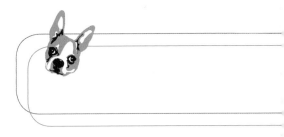

ACID JAZZ

There are great DJs and musicians out there who specialize in doctoring up existing jazz songs and layering them with funk and hip-hop beats to create a genre called acid jazz—this really works well at daytime events like brunches or early hour cocktail parties with a mellow vibe. This style of music has a pulsing beat that keeps the energy flowing without falling into dance territory. It has a sexy, loungey, relaxed feel that goes well in many restaurants and lounges as well because you can still talk over it. I love the *Jazzmatazz* series of albums featuring Guru and Japanese acid jazz artist Gota.

AIR FRESHENER

Why is it that every aerosol air freshener somehow ends up in my mouth? It's not enough that I am dealing with the smell of feces, but the cover-up smell of ocean breezes is simply too much. "Just light a match" is actually right on target for chasing away offensive odors in the bathroom. A lit match releases sulfur dioxide, which is a strong enough smell to beat back any odor. The only problem with matches is their fleeting life span—ideally, you want something to stick around for a while. So keep the fires burning with incense in a natural scent like jasmine, sage, or lavender—not something contrived like banana split or bubble gum. My favorite brand of good-smelling stuff these days is Voluspa (www .voluspacandles.com), which has magnificent candles, incense, and other fragrance items. Subtle scents are the way to go (conversely, I can tell if there is a Votivo candle burning a mile away). In a bathroom, a strong-smelling candle will end up (to put it bluntly) smelling like poop-covered flowers, and who wants that? The new kid in home fragranceville is reed diffusers—those pretty bottles filled with scented oil and an array of reeds resembling pickup sticks. The oil permeates the wood and it scents the room with a balanced, light effect. And my last pick of air fresheners is the Native Americanesque bundle of dried sage. Just light the end of a sage stick, let it smolder on a fire-safe plate, and your whole world will smell like heaven. You can get sage bundles in places where hippies hang out, like health food stores or aromatherapy spas.

AIR WALL

Air walls are usually found in hotel ballrooms that are extremely large and can be broken up into smaller spaces. Air walls actually fold up like an accordion within the walls of the space, and they roll out on a tracking system when needed. They are engineered to inhibit sound disturbances between the spaces and are usually fairly neutral in appearance. They are also useful in creating storage areas that can go unnoticed by guests, like coat-check areas or production zones.

ALABASTER

Beyond the type of skin we'd all die for, alabaster is a gorgeous surface that can add easy elegance to your celebration. Alabaster is a mineral that comes in many forms—one piece of it is never the same as the next. Thanks to its natural amber-hued veins, alabaster provides a warm pink glow when light is shone through it. I have often used wall sconces, lamp shades, and votive candleholders made out of alabaster for this reason.

Because alabaster has the richness and sophistication of marble, but with a lighter and more contemporary feel, it's often used for countertops or bar tops, vases, and wall sections as well. It's expensive and fragile, but one of the most noticeable and stunning elements in a room. Alabaster can be found at most local marble, stone, and tile stores.

ALUMINUM FOIL

I'm not suggesting you sculpt swans out of foil for your guests' leftovers (ahh, the eighties)—but you can use it for place mats, wall coverings, gift wrap, and even a sculptural chandelier! Aluminum foil is the poor man's bling and can have the same effect as costlier rhinestone or crystal accents. The great thing about foil is that it's reflective and malleable. Whether your room is lit with a cool blue, a warm amber, or a fierce red, foil casts it beautifully.

You can make huge foil balls for buffet table accents (rest them on the tabletop or in the mouths of tall vases or hang them with fishing line from the ceiling), or work smaller versions of them into table centerpieces. To make it even cheaper, you can buy large amounts from industrial kitchen suppliers.

AMARANTHUS

This is the sexiest-ugliest flower on earth—some people hate it, others adore it. This flower has a droopy appearance kind of like Spanish moss or seaweed, but it's a bit more voluptuous. Its stem starts out stalky and straight, but the tip of the flower curves and dips downward. Amaranthus comes in hanging and nonhanging varieties in deep burgundy red or chartreuse green. This flower adds a lot of texture—we've covered ceilings with hanging amaranthus, which makes the space look like it's dripping with lush dreadlocks Bob Marley style. (Other great ceiling flowers are grapevine, wisteria, jasmine vine, and English ivy—anything that has a stable continuous stem you can hang it with.) Amaranthus also looks phenomenal dripping from the bottom part of a tall branch arrangement like a droopy collar. Sometimes I like to do paradoxical pairings by grouping it with lush romantic blooms like peonies. Amaranthus is also hardy, which is important at an event. Flowers have to withstand a lifetime of slings and arrows at a party, but this one takes a licking.

AMBER BULBS

When a room is washed in a soft amber light, you automatically get a roomful of good-looking people (at least in photos). In the industry, we call it soap opera lighting. When people feel beautiful, they relax their inhibitions. That's why it's smart to make the dance floor lighting really sexy and low so people don't get embarrassed by their ridiculous moves. These lighting rules even

apply to your home: Try adding a soft amber bulb in one of the bathrooms—though perhaps not the one you apply your makeup in. When guests are over for dinner, they'll go in there and feel gorgeous.

AMENITIES

Here's my dream list of things to include in your bathroom for your guest's convenience. Think of it this way: The more doodads you offer them, the less they will rifle through your medicine cabinet!

- Hand soap
- Hand lotion
- Refreshing face spray, like those Evian spray bottles
- Kleenex
- Antacids
- Clear nail polish to fix runs in stockings or to stop a chip on a nail
- Mints or breath freshener
- Hair brush or comb
- Bobby pins/safety pins—lots of them!
- Band-Aids

- Eyedrops
- Advil
- Hair ties
- Matches
- Deodorant
- Antibacterial gel for hands
- Perfume
- Feminine products, like tampons and panty liners

ANTIQUES/ARTWORK

Whether your event is taking place in your home or at a venue, there will surely be items there that have great value and need to be protected. Obviously things are at risk when you fill a room with people, especially if they choose to flail about or drink heavily, so don't be ashamed of wanting to safeguard your belongings. The secret to preventing red wine spills on that vintage white shag carpet or Knoll sofa is to simply remove it from your event. You many be thinking, What the hell will people sit on? And where do I hide this stuff in my five-hundred-square-foot apartment?

Well, there are many options. You can rent temporary furniture from a local prop warehouse; it's insured so you aren't responsible for wreckage. You can rent temporary storage space or hire local movers to hold fine artwork on their truck overnight in a secure and guarded parking area. (Be sure to only hire movers that are bonded and insured.) If you are nervous about bare walls, a great lighting designer can fill that void by lighting the walls with simple patterns or beams of complementary colors. Or you could temporarily slipcover your existing furniture. With retailers like Pottery Barn and IKEA, slipcovers are available for many styles of sofas and chairs. You can also go to a local fabric mart and estimate the yardage you will need to cover your furniture. If you go this route, you need to make sure the fabric is flame retardant.

ASHTRAYS

Let's face it, when people are partying, they sometimes want to smoke. The truth is there is still a huge population that lights up—cigars, cigarettes, joints—and these people deserve to come to your event. We all know what secondhand smoke can do, so designate smoking areas in a completely separate part of your house or venue. By providing these areas, you are protecting your stuff from unsightly burn holes or even from catching fire. I must see about twenty-five burn holes per sofa in most of the clubs and venues I have worked in, and frankly, it ain't pretty. The smell factor can be pretty intense as well. When creating a smoking area, I tend to make it a somewhat undesirable place to be without being a total jerk about it. Outside setups make the most sense; if it's cold outside, you'd think that people would stay away, but I am amazed at how many people brave the cold for a ciggie. If a smoking area is near a white or light-colored wall, that wall will discolor after a few events. Drapes are also catching mitts for these types of stains, so keep fabrics away. The most ideal smoking zones have concrete floors studded with many sand-filled ashtrays that are emptied during the events. Place enough ashtrays in these areas to prevent people from throwing their butts on the ground or off a rooftop. The ultimate outdoor ashtrays are simply made from sand in buckets. What I love about sand is that you can bury the evidence, like a cat in the litterbox. The sand is also a number one fire extinguisher. Sand can be bought at a hardware store or nursery. I often use small buckets of sand for door props when throwing indoor/outdoor parties, and you can even stick incense in the sand to keep the cigarette areas smelling somewhat pleasant.

ASTROTURF

AstroTurf lives outside your favorite sports arena, and it comes in more colors than shocking green. In the event world, AstroTurf is often used as flooring in a tent or to cover a gymnasium surface or parking lot. It's available in different lengths and can beautifully mimic real grass if need be. Many times we have produced large outdoor events with hosts who were very worried about the state of the lawn postevent. AstroTurf is here to save the day. Fine artificial turf can also be used to fill in balding areas of your lawn— just match the shade of green. When you wish the floor would just disappear, black turf doesn't interrupt the decor. AstroTurf is waterproof, hardy, and easily cut to whatever size you need. It is also fun to use the higher-end grass blade stuff as a buffet table topper or centerpiece: Place a square of it in a low, square glass vase and arrange single stems of premium cut florals in it—or just the flower heads if you prefer.

ATTIRE

Terms like black tie seem obvious, but people often wonder, "Does that mean that I have to wear a black tie?" It is confusing these days: Men can wear a gorgeous black suit with a monochromatic shirt and tie, or a single-breasted black suit with a bow or straight tie. Both are acceptable at a black-tie event, as is the more traditional tuxedo. With women, I have noticed that black tie conjures up one thing: a black dress. This is disappointing because formal attire is a lot broader than we have been conditioned to think. It just means dress as nicely as you can. Black tie is a more conservative atmosphere— therefore, shoes not sneakers, boobs should be kept under wraps, and hair and makeup should be not too over the top. But that doesn't mean that you can't bring a little bit of your personal style to the outfit. Guys can wear outrageous cufflinks or funky striped socks that peek out only when they are seated. Men's fashion designer Paul Smith offers amazing accessories for this purpose. Women have more choices: a fabulous broach, cool hair accessories, and of course great shoes and clutches. A moisturizer with a bit of sparkle in it across the upper chest and neck can look quite magical.

When you're inviting people you know well, you can create your own attire. I've seen casual chic used a lot in regard to dress. Simply, casual chic for men means that it's fine to wear a coat, no tie, an open collar, and a great pair of jeans—but no flip-flops. Flip-flops are casual but not chic. The same rules apply for women, but if the flip-flops happen to have grown a nice wedge heel, I will lay down my sword. Girls can get away with a lot more in the dress code arena simply because we have so many options. We can wear a cotton halter dress with some chandelier earrings, but if a guy wears a simple cotton shirt, he needs to at least accessorize with a good pair of shoes. Casual chic also does not give you license to dress like a slut. We have thrown events ranging from Bohemian chic to cocktail fabulous to simply white. On that note, you can demand that your guests wear one color to your party, but keep in mind that at least half the people might not be so happy to comply. Guys find it relieving to be told what to wear, but women think that being forced to wear white on a fat day is the kiss of death.

AWNINGS

If you want indoor and outdoor flow for your guests at your house party, then awnings are a nice touch. Your guests can still sit and relax outdoors with the covering of an awning, and they don't need to be permanent fixtures in your home. You can buy temporary awnings that hook onto your house with rope and an anchor (as this option isn't cheap, you may as well make them permanent if you like the look of them). You can even get them James Bond–style, remote controlled and retractable. Awnings can be made by a window treatment center—I have even enlisted sail-making craftsmen to make my party awnings!

BACK BAR

A small table set up behind the bar to be used as an extra production space for cutting lemons, refilling the ice bucket, storing extra glasses, and keeping your bar tools, such as your wine openers and such. This way you can save the display area for your drink selection, your signature cocktail description, and some cocktail napkins.

BRANCHES

Branches sit beautifully in a vase, crawl up the sides of a stairwell, and create gorgeous archways. You can hang votives from them, and if they don't give forth flowers naturally, I've been known to wire blooms onto them.

CITRONELLA CANDLES

These candles are the ultimate multitaskers. Much like cavemen evolving into today's metrosexual, the old bug spray has evolved into citronella candles, those mood-setting, light-giving decorations that deter bugs that are trying to crash your party. Citronella candles are great additions to any outdoor or open-house party. Citronella comes in a variety of forms: tiki torches that stake right into the yard, which you can use around the perimeter of your event; buckets to create pathways on dark properties to help people get around; and small votive candles that can double as part of your decor. The smell of a citronella candle is mildly citrusy and pleasant to most folks' noses—but not to mosquitoes.

COLOR BLOCKS

Say you have a large, loft-style room. Break up the space by decking one corner of the room (furniture, flowers, rugs, or lighting) in ranges of orange, and another corner in violet or purple tones from light lavender to deep amethyst. Your guest will have a different emotional reaction depending on the hue they are surrounded in: red can express a sexy feeling, orange or yellow produces a happy and elated feeling, black is sleek and sexy, and white is clean and contemporary. Color blocks are a great way to add adventure within a room without breaking the bank by physically building different points of interest.

CORKAGE FEE

A corkage fee is when you bring in a different type of wine than what the venue offers. The owners aren't making a profit from someone else's wine, so they need to charge you a corkage fee for each bottle of wine or each person they serve. Common corkage fees span from $10 to $20 per person.

CUPCAKES

By now I think we've all already seen the tiered plate filled with cupcakes looking like a huge scrumptious cake, but despite its ubiquity, these little devils are more diverse than one would imagine. Go beyond chocolate and vanilla and get creative with flavor. Start with a good

old-fashioned chocolate cupcake but rock its world by creating a pomegranate or fresh mint icing. Get crazy and frost the entire cupcake instead of just the tops (don't worry, I'm sure you will figure out a way to get the icing off your fingers). In the summer months, create icebox cupcakes by filling cupcake pans with layers of chocolate wafer cookies and sweet whipped cream or custard, and top them off with chocolate shavings or cocoa powder. Cupcakes can be used as tasty parting gifts for those driving-home-munchies because they are compact, easy to wrap, and seem to make us all giddy and childlike.

DANCE FLOOR

As I've mentioned before, the most important part of creating a dancing space is to dim all the lights, as Donna Summer sang. Try to use a part of the floor that will not collapse if people dance on it, and keep in mind that certain harder surfaces can have your guests bending over

in agony the next morning (and resenting the whole party), so if you have concrete or wood floors, consider purchasing some thin office-floor matting (check out Staples, OfficeMax, or Home Depot) that will protect your floor and your guests' bodies. If you are dealing with a plush or shag carpet, I would suggest rolling it up or putting matting on top of it. Women's heels can practically knit their own sweaters while dancing—not good. If you have a handy friend, it's great to be able to build a raised dance floor that can rest on a plywood platform. Then you can paint or lay black-and-white linoleum tile on top for a checkered floor, or use any pattern you want. You can also build a platform out of acrylic or fiberglass (a little more advanced, so bring in the professionals for this one) and wire fluorescent lights into it that you can gel to a specific color. Then you've got a *Saturday Night Fever* light-up dance floor, which is pretty impressive stuff. Make sure to test any dance floor with a few dry runs to ensure its stability before injuring all your friends.

DIE-CUT

A die-cut process involves cutting irregular shapes in paper with a die tool—this is usually an extravagant cost if you get it custom made. However, a bunch of premade die-cut invitations out there are affordable.

ELECTRICITY DROPS

Electricity drops or boxes supply electricity wherever you need it, even if there is no outlet nearby and you need more power than a regular extension cord can provide. They should only be installed by an electrician; this is grown-up shit and you should not attempt to do this on your own. If you just need some power across the room so you can plug in your iPod dock, then use an extension cord, but make sure the cord is placed behind furniture or secured with electrical tape in areas where people could trip over it. Gaffing tape is usually laid first on sensitive areas like wood floors because it's not very sticky and will not ruin nice surfaces. The cord can go on top of the gaffing tape, and then heavy-duty duct tape goes over that to hold it securely in place. These tapes can be purchased at your hardware store and come in a variety of colors.

ENGRAVING

Engraving is a painstaking printing process, and customers pay dearly for it. Engraved invitations have distinctive raised lettering and a "bruise" on the backside of the paper (a faint impression). Old-school companies like Crane, Dempsey & Carroll, and Cartier can offer traditionally formal designs, but there are a lot of more modern, whimsical engraving companies, like Luella Press (luellapress.com) and Prentiss Douthit (prentissdouthit .com). If you like the look of engraving but can't afford the prices, there's thermography, sometimes called poor man's engraving because the type also appears raised off the page, but it's far more economical.

FAKE FENG SHUI

My personal definition of feng shui: an environment that is harmoniously balanced, one that is defined by the individual(s) creating it. To be clear, this should be an environment that evokes a (hopefully positive) emotion when people enter it and that will remain in their memory well after they have left. To fake feng shui balance, it's key that you direct the flow of the room. Lounge seating should be placed perpendicular to the wall rather than up against it so seated people have a view of the room, and at no time should their back be to other people. The idea is that all people are a part of the party!

FAUX STRIPED WALLPAPER

This faked look can be achieved in a few ways: Find a striped pattern on the Internet, have it re-created at Kinko's life-size, and tack it up, or you can paint faux stripes on the walls using painter's tape and different colors. Just make sure you keep your lines straight!

FEATHERS

I adore feathers. Peacock, quail, or ostrich, these natural beauties bring texture and mystique to many bouquets, centerpieces, boutonnieres, passed-tray accents, clothing, and hair bling. A simple tall vase filled with pure white ostrich feathers is twice as stunning as a centerpiece filled with every premium flower. They are perfect for wedding accents: For the gentlemen who can't stand wearing a traditional boutonniere on his lapel, a small, neutral-toned quail feather is always a welcome alternative. Try using a small nosegay of feathers near the bustle of your wedding dress or placing a few feathers into a bridal bouquet instead of using a filler berry or flower.

FEE PEE

I use this term to describe those postevent surprise costs that hit us like an early period in white pants. Sometimes when working with vendors or rental companies, magical little charges haunt us afterward, such as for cleaning, parking tickets, extra food runs, fuel surcharges, or hidden service fees. Your local liquor store clerk says, "Sure, no problem—we'll deliver it for you," and then you get a bill a month later for that delivery. Fee pee can make you resent ever having had the event in the first place, but it's easy to avoid if you communicate constantly with your vendors and ask them what all costs are up front. Politely ask them if they will charge for the extra service they are so generously offering. Your miscellaneous budget should cover this, unless you need it to bail one of your guests out of jail or something.

FISHING WIRE

This is a wonderful material that can be used for so much more than the catch of the day. Fishing wire (or line) comes in a variety of weight strengths up to two hundred pounds. We often use it to hang things like paper lanterns, signage, votives, and even piñatas. Since fishing line is made out of clear nylon, it's pretty invisible, which helps give the appearance of things floating in air. It can be found at any hardware store, Home Depot, and, obviously, a bait and tackle shop!

FLAME-RETARDANT FABRIC

Kind of obviously, this is a type of fabric that has been treated so it's resistant to fire. If you are creating temporary draping or slipcovers for your party, using flame-retardant fabric is simply the smart way to go. You shouldn't use this fabric only in areas where you have candles or people are smoking, because if there is a fire at your event, the flames will move quickly, even if it's fifty feet or more away. Personally, I think if you're having an event that has a designated outdoor smoking area and not a lot of indoor candlelight, then using this kind of fabric could be expensive and time consuming. But you can never be too safe, and most rental venues require that you provide fire-retardant fabric and certificates of proof. This type of treatment should be professionally handled (as in, don't try this at home!). You can buy fabrics that are already treated from your local fabric store; if you need to have fabric treated, the store clerk should be able to point you in the right direction.

FLAT PRINTING

This is the more minimal approach to printing—no pressing plates and carving into copper—but a lovely choice nonetheless. Some of my favorite smaller companies that offer this style of printing with a unique aesthetic are Wiley Valentine (wileyvalentine.com), Mainio (mainiostyle.com), and B. T. Elements (btelements.com).

FLOOR CUSHIONS

You can make floor cushions out of beanbags or memory foam—just make sure they are big and firm enough to handle all types of loads and are water- and weatherproof. Always provide a low table as well for folks to deposit their food and drinks.

FLORAL FOAM

A spongy substance, floral foam holds water and its shape. Just sink the foam in water to let the block absorb all the liquid, and place stems in it so the flowers have enough to drink. The foam comes in blocks mostly, but also in other shapes like igloos (for round arrangements) and in plastic cages, which you can affix to surfaces such as chuppahs or even funeral caskets.

FOOD SAFETY

Don't go overboard on refrigerating foods. Don't freak out about foods sitting out on the counter or buffet table for a while—they are stronger than you think. Milk is fine for quite some time left out at room temperature, and things like mayonnaise that are said to be really fragile are already so processed to begin with that a seat on the counter won't make it go bad. If one person claims food poisoning from your event and not all twenty of your guests do, then more than likely that person just drank too much.

However, do beware of cross-contamination while you are preparing food. Use separate cutting boards and knives for produce and meat, and always wash your hands after handling raw meat, fiddling with flowers, or wrestling with your dog.

FURNITURE RENTALS

Using furniture rentals allows you to completely change your environment with no commitment. Say you want to create a comfy seating lounge at your venue, or that even though you adore your farmhouse in the country, you want to exude a much more modern feel at your event with midcentury furniture at your event. There are furniture rental places in practically every town—some may not cater to events and are more for transient people in temporary corporate housing, but it has been my experience that even these types are open to event rental deals too. Remember to read your contracts carefully and take note of the deposit cost and cleaning fees!

GEEKY NECESSITIES

When I go to an event, my black backpack is filled with vital items such as the party timeline, a vendor contact list, emergency numbers of the local police or fire station, lipstick, lip balm, and makeup for touchups, breath freshener, a snack bar, walkie-talkie, an extra battery for a walkie-talkie, cell phone charger, a calculator, a flashlight, some Band-Aids, deodorant, a flicker for lighting candles, and three pens (in case the other two don't work).

GEL

A gel is a colored film of plastic to place over a light source to change the hue of a room. You can buy gels at music stores like Guitar Center or at wholesale lighting places.

GOBO

A gobo is a stencil made out of a heat-resistant metal and placed over a lighting fixture so a pattern is projected onto a surface. Gobos have been responsible for many a wow factor at my past events: projecting a company logo on the outside of a building, a name on the entrance floor, or even a phrase like *Happy Birthday!* in the middle of a swimming pool. Gobos have to be custom made by lighting professionals; to find them in your area, just Google it. If this gets too complicated and you don't want to involve professionals, then I suggest using a relatively simpler custom stencil design on the walls to get the same effect (see Stencils).

HOT SPOTS

In these areas of a room the music is either too loud or too soft because of the the way the room was constructed. You should always walk completely around a room when doing a sound check to make sure that the sound is even, no matter where you're standing.

HOTELS

So many different types of hotels are out there—the ultracool, trendy boutique hotel (where you may feel at home but your parents may be mortified by its "weirdness"), your average large-scale, chain hotel, your old-school hotel filled with grand stairwells and chandeliers and the faint smell of mothballs, and then the "little bit of both" hotels—which are an ideal compromise for your guests. A hotel chain that comes easily to mind in this category are the W Hotel properties—I like the fact that they have trendy, organic, and homey elements all at once in most of their locations. When booking a hotel for your event, you need to keep in mind the same considerations you would when choosing any venue plus a few more. If your guests will be staying overnight, check out what the rooms are like. Are the restaurants user friendly for all age groups, is the hotel kid friendly, does the room rate the hotel offers seem feasible for most of your guests, is the location of the hotel desirable, easy to get to, and allow your guests to explore a nearby neighborhood that is safe and interesting? Other things to look into:

1. Is the hotel event-friendly? Do people regularly throw parties here, and does the hotel have a designated full-time events coordinator on staff who will be in charge of your party from day one?

2. Is it a union hotel? If it is, the staff will work only certain hours, and most of the production of your event will have to go through them, like dealing with electricity, hanging decorations or fabric, and staging for entertainment. Even though you may want to hire an event designer or lighting engineer who does not normally work for the hotel, you may be forced to go with the hotel's in-house union members, and you will have to work according to their strict timeline. Being part of a union means there are more rules and guidelines to follow.

3. Will the other hotel guests be able to view your party? Try to make sure that the hotel blocks off a special bank of elevators or the entrance to the party. The hotel should also provide some in-house security to keep out crashers.

4. What comes with your event package? Hotels often offer a free night in the hotel for the guest(s) of honor or an upgrade of some sort, and a special room rate for your guests. Do you and your guests get discounts on food or other amenities such as the fitness center or spa treatments? What exactly is included in the pricing for the event itself? For example, are the room, tables, linens, waitstaff, votive candles, and staging all covered? (See also Room Blocks.)

ICE

Ice is a beautiful thing so I wholeheartedly recommend working its good looks into your bar display. I like to let a layer of ice freeze on my vodka bottles by submerging them in a clear bucket I've thrown crushed rose petals or pomegranate seeds into with the water. Freeze the bucket and pull out the frozen vodka Popsicle after a couple hours. The accents cluster at the bottom but it still looks pretty in the clear receptacle, and keeps your liquor cold too! I usually avoid adding things to ice cubes, though. It's strange to have floaters in your drink once the ice melts. But a frozen garnish can be stunning on a shallow tray or in an ice bucket.

INSURANCE

The first things that spring to mind with insurance are usually little niggling things like your home, car, *life*—but believe it or not, there is event insurance too, and it's definitely worth looking into. Event insurance protects you if one of your guests decides to place a curtain on top of a lit candle for the hell of it. Things happen when people are celebrating—wine gets spilled, hot wax mysteriously works its way out of its candleholder, and food somehow finds its way onto couch cushions. You can call your regular insurance provider and ask if you can buy a certificate of insurance just for your event. Depending on where you are having the party, the amount required to insure the event will vary anywhere from $1,500 to $6 million, and the price of your certificate will reflect that. If you are hiring vendors, they should all provide a certificate of insurance for you—especially a caterer who is providing liquor. Find out what type of insurance is required by your venue, and add that in your budget costs.

JIGGER

This is that small, usually stainless-steel, double-sided measuring cup bartenders use to get the right amount of alcohol into your drinkie-drink. One side measures a perfect 1.5 ounce shot; the other measures a smaller 1 ounce pony shot. Jiggers are useful if you are a novice bartender and you're mixing a martini or something equally potent—leave the eyeballing to the professionals.

LADIES' TEA

The ladies' tea party has been around for eons, and it has grown from a gathering of proper gentlewomen dressed to the nines discussing society matters or literature to a gaggle of girls having a rowdy martini lunch at a trendy restaurant. Ladies' teas can take place in a living room, a hotel suite, around a swimming pool, or on a fabulous city rooftop. Instead of getting blitzed and bloated, it's nice to leave most of the room for conversation—indulge in small bites like finger sandwiches or individual fruit tarts. Tea has come such a long way too. These days, you don't have to serve an Earl Grey—sample an enormous variety of Japanese green teas, chai, yerba maté—even bubble tea! A ladies' tea should not leave women exhausted and spent but rather inspired and ready to get on with the rest of their day.

LAWN

Before throwing an outdoor party on your lawn, take a few precautions to preserve its lush green goodness. First: Make sure you turn your sprinkler system off a good seventy-two hours preparty so you don't inadvertently create a natural Slip 'N Slide in your backyard. Treat your lawn with an organic flea or bug pesticide found in local nurseries or garden shops to prevent colonies of bugs from attending your event. If vendors' or rental supplies will be delivered on your lawn, protect it by laying down tarp or sheets of light plywood—heavy rentals like sound equipment and the like can tear up your grass.

Manicure the lawn so it looks pretty by mowing and filling in patchy areas with fresh-looking sod you can buy in two-foot squares from the nursery. Your lawn has a memory—if something horrible happens to it during the event, it may show up later in its growth pattern. Afterward, let it recover by staying off it for a bit and giving it plenty of water and food.

LED LIGHTS

If you are having an event in a windy place like a tent or a home with open windows, having to relight your roomful of candles every five minutes can drive a host crazy. That's where LED lights come in. An LED light (for light-emitting diode) is a small, powerful light that is powered by a tiny battery. The LED light is a great alternative to candlelight and even comes in a flame-shaped votive style so when it's in a holder, it's hard to tell it's not real. Many other forms include tiny single lights whose battery is activated by pulling a string; LEDs in long thin strips that are great for lining pathways or for placing under tables or bars so they can glow through a table linen; and multiple LEDs housed in small boxes that can be operated by remote control for cycling different colors. This is fabulous new lighting technology that helps make most of my events one of a kind. LEDs can be used in a gazillion ways: Hide them in a floral arrangement, put them at the bottom of a vase mixed with rocks so it glows from within, use them under place cards on an escort table so each card is backlit, or even put one in a hanging paper lantern. LEDs can sometimes be found in craft stores such as Michael's or a floral supply store—or just Google them! They are expensive—they cost a minimum of $2 per light and usually come in packs of ten—but they last much longer than incandescent bulbs and use much less energy. We once hung three thousand LED lights in jars from the ceiling of a tent and it looked like a sky full of fireflies—it was magical.

LETTERPRESS

Letterpressed invitations and greeting cards are very popular right now, and a bunch of small letterpress companies are churning out some adorable ones. A few companies I love: Hello Lucky (hellolucky.com), Oblation (oblationpapers.com), Elum (elumdesigns.com), Alee and Press (Aleeandpress.com), Smock (smockpaper.com), Egg Press (eggpress.com), and Dauphine Press (dauphinepress.com).

LOFTS

Events opened up a whole new world of economic possibilities to loft owners about twenty years ago—a little added income for a cavernous space, perfect for parties. Usually lofts are only an option when you live in a larger city with industrial buildings that have been converted for residential use. When renting a loft for an event, start by Googling loft event rentals in your city, or look in a telephone directory for photo studios, which tend to be all-white, clean, and used to a certain amount of production wear and tear. Larger raw spaces also tend to be in neighborhoods that are more industrial and less apt to have noise restrictions. Start calling around and asking if a space can legally hold events. It's best for a loft to have an on-site event manager, someone who will be there throughout to make sure the event runs smoothly.

Also, it's helpful to see pictures of past events to ensure that the loft management has sufficient experience. As far as budget is concerned, be aware that most lofts do not have in-house items such as tables and chairs or multiple bathrooms, so be sure to include any of these as added expenses.

LOMEY DISH

The clear plastic Lomey dish comes in different sizes, from four inches to twelve inches in diameter. These dishes are great at disappearing—when you use them in floral arrangements, the arrangement looks as if it's floating on the table. You can also use them as water retainers in conjunction with less-practical containers, by arranging florals in the Lomey dish and placing it on top of a candelabra or vase.

MAGNETS

I used to think this was a really cheesy way to go, but I must say one thing: When we sent magnets

as STDs (save the dates), a higher rate of attendees remembered to come to the party than with all other modes of notification. Magnets hang around, gently reminding guests of your party every time they go to the fridge for a snack (which, in my house, is about seventy-two times a day). Magnets can be custom designed and sent in normal envelopes as long as they're within weight requirements. However, I suggest using padded envelopes or at least some wrapping in protective tissue. Those things could stick to other things if not padded a little—you don't want them sticking to the side of some mailbox somewhere and never making it to their destinations.

MICROWAVE

The microwave can be a great helper for any host, but you have to be sure not to overcook the food—it should be used only to quickly heat up something. Never use for bread or dough products (it makes them tough and inedible) or anything that needs to be crispy—those need to be warmed in the oven or toaster oven.

MONITOR SPEAKERS

These are the speakers that face the musicians onstage, so the performers can hear what they are doing over the din of the party. The white noise of a room makes it difficult for musicians to hear whether they are in tune, so this is an integral part of a live band's setup.

MONOCHROMATIC COLOR SCHEME

This color scheme works with every shade of one color. So if you are using blue as your palette, you could use the lightest, almost-white blue all the way to midnight-sky dark blue—the shade you choose doesn't matter, because everything in the palette will harmonize perfectly. A good way to visualize this kind of color scheme is by looking at the subtle hue changes on paint chips. Using monochromatic palettes

avoids busyness and visual clutter in a room. The same rules apply to flower arrangements: Pick just one color and put several types of flowers in that color in the same vase. I believe that monochromatic palettes train the eye to focus on the beauty of the individual elements you're using, instead of making your guests dizzy with options.

MOROCCAN

Morocco! Just the word conjures up visions of the exotic and faraway. Most of us have never been there, so it's probably time to use your imagination when coming up with the details for this kind of party. Picture lush pillow lounges where people recline, idly eating from overflowing platters of oranges, dates, and pistachios. Create your own hookah lounge by ordering a hookah on the Internet with luscious fruit tobacco, and let your guests experience something novel. Buy four-post trellis structures from Smith & Hawken, Target, or any

garden store, pop them in your backyard, throw some mosquito netting or fabric over them, and voilà! You have little tents that are still open to the rest of the party. You can have food in one, a hookah lounge in the other, a tarot card reader, a henna tattoo artist, or even a cigar tasting area. If you want to get literal about Morocco, obviously you should do your research and pick out elements that you think you can somehow express in a digestible fashion for your guests.

OUTDOOR HEATER

Providing outdoor heaters allows your guests to enjoy a slightly chilly evening and not have to squeeze themselves indoors just to regain blood circulation. These heat lamps operate much like a barbecue grill by using a small petroleum tank that rests in the base and feeds the fire that radiates out of the top. You can regulate the level of heat; these babies can really roast everyone in the immediate area, so start off on low and raise the temperature as necessary. Just like anything that has to do with fire, it's best to place heat lamps on a nonfiber surface—not on rugs, indoors, or even on grass that can get easily singed. The ideal place for a heat lamp is on a stone or concrete patio. You can buy heat lamps from restaurant supply stores, barbecue grill providers, hardware or home furnishing stores, and you can even get them from an event rental company.

OUTDOOR LIGHTING

It's just as important for your guests to be able to see outside as it is inside. Obviously you don't want to have to scatter reading lamps all over your yard, and thankfully there are many nice outdoor lighting options for you. I love solar-powered lights. Not only are they good for the environment, but these things really work! You can buy perimeter lights on stakes that go in the ground at any Home Depot or gardening store; they hang out during the day, soaking up energy, and when the sun sets, they magically light right up. They are weather resistant, come in heavy plastic or metal (depending on how much you want to spend), and are an innovative way to avoid wiring up your backyard. String lights are also wonderful for creating a festive landscape. If you have lots of trees or deck areas, run an extension cord from your house, string the lights in the trees or around the periphery, and create an outdoor wonderland that not only provides light but decoration as well. String lights are way better than the ye olde Christmas tree variety—now they come in a gazillion styles, shapes, and colors, and you can find them year-round at many stores like Smith & Hawken, Target, Kmart, and hardware stores. A great way to ensure that your lights stay put in your trees or deck areas is to use zip ties to keep them in place. You can always take the lights down postevent, but they're great to have around even if it's just you sitting outside after dinner, spacing out. Paper lanterns are also a nice soft touch—the paper diffuses the light beautifully. Plus they are dirt cheap—as low as a buck per light from places like Cultural Intrigue (culturalintrigue.com) and Pearl River (pearlriver.com). IKEA, Pottery Barn, and Smith & Hawken also sell paper lanterns during their summer sales. (Paper lanterns also look great indoors, hanging above a dinner table.) Also look for lanterns in fabrics like silk or canvas.

PAR CANS

Par cans are containers that hold a flood light. They can sit on the floor and shoot a beam of light up a wall creating a lit perimeter in your party room. Using several of these in one space can really help "glow" a room.

PER HEAD FEE

If there is an in-house caterer at your venue, the price is determined by a per head fee, meaning the cost of food, service, tables, chairs, and bar for each person is included in this price. In my East Coast/West Coast experience, average per head fees in a high-end venue will run anywhere from $140 to $250 per person. If the venue doesn't have an in-house caterer, you can bring in your own—then you'll be paying a venue fee only and the catering, rentals, bar, and service will be tallied separately.

PERMITS

Permits are little pieces of paper that can be a pain in the ass to obtain but tell the world that you're allowed to do what you're doing. Most permits involve parking, like when you need extra space on your street for vehicles so you ask the city to give you written permission to block off the area. If you want to have an event in a public area such as a park or beach, you also need the city's permission to do so (and a certificate to prove it). Many times no one even shows up to see if you have the correct permit, but don't tempt fate. If you don't have that little piece of paper, the authorities can completely shut you down. When planning an event at your home, call the chamber of commerce to find out what you should do to throw a "clean" party. When renting a venue, ask the staff what the permit requirements are for that space.

PIPE AND DRAPE

Sometimes called pipe and plate, pipe and drape consists of heavy floor plates with extendable vertical poles attached (usually eight to twelve feet high). A crossbar connects the poles, and you can hang a sleeve of fabric (the drape) from that to create a fabric wall. Party rental places offer these, and most rentals come in ten-foot sections and are about $17 to $25 per section. If you don't like the fabric that comes with the rental, you can always sew your own drape, or drape your fabric over the existing one. Gather the fabric in the middle with a tassel so it has the dramatic look of a curtained entrance. You can also hang a favorite shower curtain from the crossbar on curtain rollers. In your home, you can fake this look by buying a tension rod and curtaining off spaces as well.

PLATING CHARGE

You may get hit with a plating charge when you bring an outside vendor, such as a wedding cake baker, to a place that has an in-house person for that service. So if you don't like the cakes your venue offers, they may charge you a plating fee for serving someone else's cake. Common plating fee charges run from $10 to $18 per person.

PLAYLIST

Basically, this is a list of songs that is prearranged and downloaded either on an MP3 player like an iPod or on a CD, so you can set your music to play at the beginning of the event and forget about it! Using a program on your computer like iTunes makes creating party playlists super easy.

PORTA-POTTY

If your home or venue is not blessed with multiple toilet options, you may want to hire extra potties, instead of letting folks into your master bath or having your outside hedge become a drunk guy dousing area. Portable toilets have come a long way from the stinky plastic cesspools of times past—now you can rent luxury toilet "suites" complete with flushable commodes, sinks, and real towels. If you live in a rural area, certain options may not be available to you through local rental companies; you may need to call your chamber of commerce to find out where you can get portables—or contact a construction company to find out who they use for their job sites. Portable potties vary in price. The basic plastic dumper will rent anywhere from $250 to $500 per day, and the deluxe, multistall trailer versions can range from $1,800 to $7,500 a day, depending on where you live. I've found that the average price for a trailer-type toilet is about $2,750, with delivery and pickup included.

POSTCARDS

Invitations and STDs (save the dates) in the form of postcards have pros and cons. On the positive side, postcards are just so simple and understated, you have to love them. They are super easy to custom design online or at a stationery store. Plus, they are sure to be read by your recipient since they don't come in a bothersome envelope. On the downside, they aren't protected by an envelope, so they are subject to harsh handling in the mail. Counteract this with a thick card stock to ensure safe delivery. The postcard may also suffer from those ugly bar code stickers the post office uses for routing that mess with your pretty design and sometimes cover up important information on the card. The economics of forgoing the envelope and higher postage is often worth going the postcard route, especially for an STD. I wouldn't take this chance, however, on a very fancy or complicated invitation because of the reasons listed above.

PROTECT SKEWERS FROM SCORCHING

Many people suggest soaking skewers in water for a half hour before grilling to avoid burning the sticks. Another way to avoid the scorch is to lay down strips of foil on the grill to protect the exposed skewer ends. But the best (cheater) way? Simply grill the ingredients off the skewer and thread them postroast!

ROAST OR TOAST

These parties are for the special people in your life, and you simply want to celebrate that. At toast parties, usually a presentation, like a slideshow or short film, lets the audience know who the people are and what they've done in their lives. This can be coupled with a dinner party where guests can offer verbal toasts to the group. We once did a wonderful toast for a well-known classical musician, and his guests (mostly musicians as well) composed an original sonata they played for him at the event. A roast tends to be the opposite in spirit, but hopefully all the jibes are in good humor. While toasters seems to be more conservative, roasters can really go to town on the guest of honor, mentioning not only the great moments in that person's life but the not-so-great ones. You may have an outspoken friend who is a wonderful person, but she may have streaked through your college graduation or won a ridiculous amount of hot-dog-eating contests—whatever! Roasting parties are more casual and have more of a storytelling atmosphere—a great starting point for a bonfire at the beach or a dinner party with an intimate group of friends. We once did a roast whose guest of honor was known for being a regular dude—a typical guy who watches sports, checks out chicks, eats pizza. His close friend found out that the honoree couldn't play football every Sunday because he volunteered at a children's cancer ward every week but never told anyone. At the roast they all poked fun at him, and then at the end they unveiled a wall constructed of beautiful notes that the children from the cancer ward had written about why they love him so much. There wasn't a dry eye in the joint. A good roast should take twists and turns throughout the evening like that one did.

ROOM BLOCK

Be careful when reserving blocks of rooms for your party guests. Hotels often ask (in the small print of course) for you to guarantee a certain number of booked rooms, and if your guests don't fulfill that guarantee, then you are liable not only for the cost of those rooms but possibly an added food and beverage charge to make up for missed-out revenue from room service and minibar options. Always ask for the group rate booker at the hotel when you call and have that person fax or e-mail you the "rules." Go over these rules with a superfine-tooth comb to ensure that you aren't liable for anything extra. I booked a room block at a fancy hotel for my wedding, and we agreed to be liable for ten rooms only, knowing that many of our friends would want to stay at a more inexpensive location. We did, however, get a discounted rate of $350, down from a normal rate of $550 per night. Also, we were told that we would get our room free if more than ten people booked rooms, which we thought was a fair deal. We listed other hotels on our Web site as options but didn't commit to any other room blocks for fear we'd be liable all over town—but we did appeal to those other hotels to give discounts to our guests if they could. We also booked our wedding during an off season, so the hotels were more than happy to have our business rather than sit empty.

SATELLITE SPEAKERS

With satellite speakers guests can hear the music at an event in multiple places at once. You may have your main stereo unit in your living room, but if you place satellite speakers around the rest of your space, including any outdoor areas, you can hear tunes from anywhere at the party. You can purchase these speakers at stores like Radio Shack and Best Buy, or rent them from a music store like Guitar Center. In terms of wiring, sometimes I think it's easier to just rent a tripod stand for the speaker to rest on rather than try to wire it into the upper corners of your room; you can always use zip ties to attach them to a balcony or deck area. Ideally, any speaker should be placed high over your guests' heads and toward the back of a space so the sound can flow into the main space.

SCENT

Earthy scents, like fig, cedar, pine, and vanilla, work well in home entertaining. For more romantic affairs, try gardenia, tuberose, or peonies. If you have a warm and sexy event, play with currants and pomegranates, or even chocolate. For a light and summery event, energizing scents like lemon, lime, grapefruit, or mandarin work well.

SCOTCHGARD

If only I could Scotchgard my whole body. This wonderful invention by 3M creates a protective and invisible shield over your fabric possessions, like your couch, pillows, and rugs. It repels liquids and doesn't let the bad stuff, like pinot noir, soak in. You can buy Scotchgard in any discount, grocery, or drugstore; this stuff has been around for ages and has proven its durability over and over again.

SHRIMP

Cooked shrimp is always a hit and unbelievably easy, as it can be prepared and chilled ahead. The biggest mistake people make is overcooking it—then you end up with rubbery or mealy shrimp, which is nasty. If you're serving shrimp cocktail, you can find very nice shrimp in the grocery aisle, precooked and frozen. In fact, all shrimp is frozen when it's delivered to grocery stores, so there is no use buying the defrosted kind in the deli case. However, in some coastal parts of the country, you can get fresh, unfrozen shrimp from seafood markets during shrimp season. Sizewise, bigger is better—look for jumbo (eleven to fifteen shrimp per pound) or extra large (sixteen to twenty shrimp per pound), or roughly shrimp weighing an ounce each. Figure on each guest eating about one-third to one-half pound.

SPECIALTY DRINK

A specialty drink adds a certain panache to any party especially if you give it a funky name like Mac Daddy Martini, Good Timez, or a salute to the guest of honor, like Carol's Cosmo. Good alcoholic foundations, I believe, are vodka, rum, or champagne. When you use something extra potent like tequila or schnapps, people just get too messed up. It's great to have your guests catch a fun party buzz, but when they start vomiting into your fish tank, it's not so fun anymore. I would also stay away from creating drinks that have an excess of sugar. Too much sugar in alcohol can cause a flurry of good times, quickly followed by a depressing crash. Ideally, what you want to achieve with a specialty drink is a concoction that guests can drink two helpings of without entering the fifth dimension and leaving the party early. Add flavor and color by mixing in fruit purees like mango, blueberry, or whatever you like. (For a puree, just buy frozen fruit and blend it to a slushy consistency.) To each glass, add two parts fruit slush to one part alcohol. It's also fun and easy to drop fresh berries into a glass of champagne and let the natural flavors blend. You can even add fresh strawberries or lemons to a pale beer for a nice twist as well. I also love this easy sangria for dinner parties: I cut up fruit—apples, grapes, mangoes, bananas—and let them soak in some wine for a few hours, then add a splash of soda water for fizziness.

STAMPS

Did you know you can actually design a custom stamp just for you? Go ahead and check out your options online at sites like zazzle .com and stamps.com. You can create stamps with an original design, a photo, a logo, or whatever makes you tick (but remember that this stuff is government run so no nudie pics!). Unfortunately between the time you design them and the time you get them in the mail, the post office will probably have upped the stamp price—so be smart and order an extra set of one- or two-cent stamps to match just in case. Depending on the company you choose, this process should only take a couple of weeks or so.

STENCILS

This is a dream product where the tough stuff is done for you! Designing a pattern for your walls is as simple as tracing, which is doable for most of us whose artistic talents petered out in third grade. Stencils usually come in cutout cardboard or heavy plastic, which makes it easy to stay within the lines and create perfect lettering or patterns. Check out the options at an art store, browse the catalog at stencil-library.com, or do an Internet search for custom stencil makers.

STONES

River stones are the most commonly used material in the event world. Rushing water wears them down and makes them shiny, smooth, and pretty. They are available in black, white, gray, brown, or red, depending on the river they come from. I like to use them at the bottom of vases or surrounding candles.

TECHNICAL RIDER

If you bring in professional musicians for your party, get a technical rider from them that explains what they are expecting outside their original contract price, such as massive amounts of orange soda, certain kinds of chairs to sit on, transportation, special equipment requirements in addition to what they're providing, extra microphones for guest speeches, and any other random request that could potentially put you into a budget tailspin.

TENTS

When people refer to tent rentals for their event, they are not talking about camping tents here—these are McMansion tents, which can take up to a week to set up and take a nice chunk out of your budget. Usually when my clients request a tented event, our first reaction is that we are dealing with high-budget people—when in fact most people simply have no idea of the

cost. The Mac Daddy tents, which average around 5,000 square feet and accommodate around a hundred people plus tables, chairs, staging, and a dance floor, can run anywhere from $3,000 to $15,000, depending on your region and the tent itself. You also need flooring for the tent so your guests are not walking on uneven ground. Subflooring goes down first—hard rubber interlocking tiles—then a simple plywood floor known as decking goes on top of that to create a hard surface you can staple any choice of carpet to (or a cheaper AstroTurf). The floor alone can run you a cool $5K to $35K depending on which carpet you choose and how big the tent is! The tent also needs four legal fire exits with visible signs and fire extinguishers. FYI, tents bring fire marshals out of the woodwork for spur-of-the-moment inspections, so be sure to follow the rules. Another extra cost is a power source for cooking, lighting, sound, and more—most likely a generator. Plus, you

may need a "back of the house" tent for any production staff. (If possible, clients often opt to give their garages to the caterer so they can do prep work indoors and walk the food to the tent if it's close by.) Then you need to light and decorate the tent so it really comes alive, and you have to hide all the mechanics, like poles and ground stakes and plastic rain flaps. Therefore, creatively draping fabric over the entire tent can take several days for a design team. If you are having a large outdoor celebration and you're worried about the weather, you should have a tent rental put aside for the week of your event in case you need it. (Most rental companies are pretty cool with waiting until about forty-eight hours before your event for you to make a decision on whether you'll be using their services.)

If you're not looking for a Barnum & Bailey–size tent, there are lesser gradients of tent partying that won't break the bank or drive you to the loony bin. For instance, I love constructing tents out of PVC piping (a strong plumber's pipe found in hardware stores), staked into soft ground and draped with a fabric canopy. Obviously, this type of tent is not as strong and won't protect you against major weather patterns, but it creates a safe place to go if a few raindrops do fall during your event. You can even take a premade, large beach tent or a large tarp camping tent and just cover it with some pretty fabric. These store-bought tents are much smaller and aren't really used for sit-down affairs but will create a safe haven for weather haters. You may also want to provide a dance floor outside, no matter what, so your guests can boogie without having to pull themselves out of a quicksand pit if it sprinkles.

TIERED PLATTERS

Tiered platters are a nice touch, even when displaying the most casual foods; the graduated appearance mimics the look of a wedding cake. These platters can be used for a multitude of items, including decorations. We once did centerpieces for a holiday party consisting of tiered platters filled with mini pottted plants—miniature rosebushes, mini succulents, and mini juniper trees. We tucked votive candles in between the plants and the whole look was lovely from all angles. You can dress a tiered platter with anything: seashells, candles, a mix of fruit and vegetables, breads and crackers—anything! You do, however, want to make sure that heavier items are displayed on the bottom tier and lighter up top to avoid a tippy situation. If you really want to get kooky, you could split the platter down the middle and do one color on the left side (like green apples) and another color on the other side (like oranges) to create a more architectural look.

TOASTS

A good toast is one with humor but not at anyone's expense. There is nothing like getting laughter out of a group to keep the party atmosphere light. I tell my hosts to steer away from talking about the past; instead, toast to the here and now and the future. It is horrible when toasters talk about past boyfriends and how screwed up a person used to be. It's better to simply say, "Here's to family and friends—and to the fact that I have both." Picking up a quote book for pithy inspiration from someone you admire (Dorothy Parker, Bill Clinton, Hannah Montana, whomever) can really help get your ideas flowing.

TRANSPORTATION FOR THE TIPSY

There is no bigger nightmare for a host than a guest's getting hurt because of drunk driving postparty. This would truly suck. So, I suggest getting really familiar with your yellow pages before the party and figure out cab options for those partyers who've had too much. You may even want to call a limousine service preevent and warn them of your date so they can ensure that plenty of cars will be available. If you have a particularly heavy-drinking crowd, it is worth the extra cost to have a car on standby for the entire evening. Most companies charge a four- or five-hour minimum so it's best to hire one that sits by the curb as guests leave and can come back to retrieve others. As Mr. T would say, don't drive drunk, fool!

VINYL DECALS

Remember how fun Colorforms were? Same idea here. Vinyl is a naturally clingy material that sticks to most surfaces with static energy, like decals on windshields or windows. You can have vinyl decals custom designed in any shape or size. They can be made by a printer or you can Google "custom vinyl decals" to find companies that can turn your art into decals. For product launches, I have used really cool vinyl runners instead of traditional ones. The best thing

about decals is that they can change your walls without damaging them. And much like a gobo, it is just a cool way to project a design onto a surface to add a splash of color to a blank wall or dance floor. Some great companies out there produce predesigned vinyl wall decals that are adhesive but fully removable, like Blik (whatisblik.com) and dVider (dvider.com). They both have a line of holiday stickers, perfect to liven up your next holiday get-together. Prices depend on what you're buying, but most of the graphic packages from both sites are around $50.

WEATHER

Mother Nature can sometimes resemble a rotten mother-in-law who drops in on you when you least expect it—so count on her showing up at your event too. Try to keep a good attitude about what you cannot control, but you certainly can take precautions to make your life a bit more flexible. You have to

have a rain contingency plan when throwing your event outdoors that goes beyond handing out umbrellas and rubber duckies. If you are set on partying outdoors, elements that can keep your party pumping are tents, awnings, heaters, and waterproof subflooring. Many people like to refer to the *Farmer's Almanac* to try determine the weather for future events, but I wouldn't put my money on the *Almanac*. The *Almanac* is good for getting estimated times for sunrises and sunsets during different seasons of the year; it's important to know when nightfall will happen to make sure your lighting is ready to spring into action.

Aside from being lovely decorative items for a summer soirée, individual hand fans are great to give guests to churn up their own refreshing breeze. Fans come in many different materials, like rattan, silk, paper, or even wood. You can find them at stores like Pearl River (pearlriver.com), on other Web sites, or you can have them custom designed. Fan prices run anywhere from $1 to $25 each. Tip: Ask to buy in bulk—it usually gets you a discount. Put them on dinner chairs, or have them on hand in large baskets so the staff can pass them around if the air gets stifling.

A word about weather and tent rentals—make sure your tent comes with removable wall options, so you can remove the walls for better airflow in a hot situation. Also, clear-sided tents tend to fog up in humid weather, so consider that depending on where you live.

WHOLESALE

Wholesale means getting the product at a price similar to what the retailer paid the manufacturer. Let's say a sofa you love was produced in China for $550. The retailer could sell it to you wholesale for close to that price. The word wholesale is kind of a sick lure at times and not always honest. Many places advertise wholesale prices on items, but there is no way of verifying that. But it's still a good word to include in your Web research to see if you can get better deals that way.

WOW FACTOR

This is that sparkling, amazing something at a party that you notice right away and leaves a big impression. Say you decide to go with a color concept and you are having an event at your home where a lot of the guests have been before. You can create a wow factor by repainting your living room in a new color—or if you think that will cause divorce, then change smaller accents like candles, area rugs, or throw pillows. By doing this, you are changing your everyday environment, which will surely make guests take notice. Here are some other wow factor ideas: Group masses of candles all in one color, or line up vases along a wall with single flowers in them. Relighting a room is a major wow factor as well—and lighting sources are movable items that can go back into hiding after your event. Call me cuckoo, but why do people always slam a floral centerpiece on the middle of the dining room table when the ceiling has beams in it and you can hang it instead with a little wood nail and some fishing wire? Or hang up votives or lanterns or piñatas. When creating a wow factor, try thinking in opposites like using black for white and front for back. Sometimes certain things will not be physically possible, but in thinking this way, you are opening your mind to the unpredictable and not-so-obvious. If your friends disown you for folding down the legs of your dining room table and providing floor cushions for a seated meal at your next dinner party, then perhaps you may want to revise your guest list!

INDEX

Italicized page references indicate illustrations.